STOP OVERTHINKING

Guide with Practical Exercises to Help Declutter Your Mind, Control Negative Thoughts and Master Your Emotions

MATILDA HART

TABLE OF CONTENTS

A GIFT FOR YOU

Thank you so much for purchasing my book!

Your support means the world to me and I'm truly honored that you have chosen to use my book as part of your self-development journey!

To show you how much I appreciate your support, here's a little thank you gift for you. A bonus audiobook version of "Stop Overthinking"

Scan the QR code below to access the Audiobook Version:

CHAPTER 1

WHAT IS OVERTHINKING?

Ah, hello there my dear reader. Welcome to the world of overthinking! Oh, wait, I mean, welcome to the world of overthinking... ugh, nevermind, you know what I mean.

If you're reading this, it's probably safe to assume that you, like me and countless others, have a bit of a tendency to overthink things. Whether it's ruminating on the past, worrying about the future, or just getting stuck in a cycle of negative thoughts, overthinking can be a real pain in the you-know-what.

But fear not, my dear reader, for this book is here to help you overcome your overthinking tendencies and live a more relaxed, stress-free life. Yes, you read that right - RELAXED. I know, it might sound like a foreign concept, but trust me, it's possible.

Throughout the chapters of this book, we'll dive into what overthinking actually is, why it happens, and most importantly, how to kick it to the curb once and for all. We'll explore techniques for mastering your emotions, turning those pesky negative thoughts into positive ones, and finding ways to destress when life feels overwhelming.

And because I know that sometimes reading about self-improvement can feel a bit overwhelming in and of itself, we've included journal prompts throughout each chapter to help you reflect and internalize what you're learning.

So buckle up, my friend and get ready to say goodbye to those pesky overthinking behaviors. It's time to take control of your mind and find your inner zen.

Overthinking is something that many of us struggle with from time to time, and it can be a real challenge to manage. You may be wondering if you're truly an overthinker, or if it's all in your head. If that's you, you may want to look at some signs that you're overthinking. A very common place that you can identify your overthinking tendencies is in daily conversations.

Firstly, you might find yourself getting stuck on the same topic or idea for a long time, going over it in your head repeatedly. This can make it hard to move on to other topics, and can even cause you to miss out on the conversation altogether. Let's look at a scenario.

Jane is having a conversation with her friend, Sarah, about their plans for the weekend. Sarah suggests that they go to a new restaurant that just opened downtown. Jane immediately starts overthinking the idea, worrying about all the possible scenarios. She wonders if the food will be good, if the restaurant will be too crowded, or if they'll be able to find parking.
As Sarah continues to talk about the restaurant and how excited she is to try it out, Jane starts to feel more and more anxious. She's so caught up in her own thoughts that she's not really listening to what Sarah is saying, and she's not contributing much to the conversation. Sound familiar?
Another sign that you might be overthinking things is if you start to feel anxious or stressed out during the conversation. This can happen if you're worrying about saying the right thing or if you're concerned about what the other person is thinking about you.

Let's say that Mark is at a job interview for his dream position. As the interviewer begins to ask him questions, Mark starts to feel his heart rate increase and his palms become sweaty.

He's worrying about how he's coming across and whether he's saying the right things. As the interview continues, Mark's anxiety levels continue to rise. He starts to stumble over his words and forget some of the key points he wanted to make. He begins to worry that he's blowing the interview and that he won't get the job.

At the end of the interview, the interviewer thanks Mark for his time and says that they'll be in touch. Mark leaves the interview feeling defeated, anxious that he didn't do well enough. He spends the next few hours replaying the interview in his head, second-guessing his responses.

These are two classic examples of overthinking, and it extends way beyond social interactions. It can happen in so many different scenarios, like work-related tasks, relationships, health concerns and decision-making. Let's go over them:

Work: Overthinking can happen when you're trying to complete a task or project at work. You worry about the quality of your work, whether it meets the expectations of your boss or colleagues, or if you're missing any important details.

Relationships: Overthinking can also happen in romantic relationships, where you constantly think about your partner's feelings, the status of the relationship or whether you're doing enough to keep the relationship strong.

Health: When you're dealing with health concerns, whether physical or mental, overthinking is especially strong. You think about the symptoms you're experiencing, the diagnosis you have received or might be given, or the treatment options available. This can lead you into a tailspin of anxiety.

Decision-making: Whether it's a small decision, like what to wear, or a big decision, like which job offer to accept, overthinking can seriously affect the way you make choices. You may freak out internally about making the wrong choice, or whether the choice you make will have any negative consequences.

In any of these scenarios, overthinking can cause stress, anxiety and can lead to indecision or inaction. If any of these scenarios apply to you, you're probably an overthinker. If you find that you're overthinking often, it might be helpful to reflect on what might be causing these thoughts. Understanding the root cause can help you develop strategies to manage overthinking and improve your mental well-being. So, what are they?

A primary, major cause of overthinking is anxiety. When you feel anxious, your mind can get stuck in a loop of worrying and ruminating, which can make it hard to focus on anything else. Overthinking can also make anxiety worse, creating a vicious cycle.

Another cause of overthinking is trauma. When you've been through a traumatic experience, your brain becomes hyper-vigilant, constantly scanning for potential threats or dangers. This can cause you to overthink situations that might not pose any threat at all.

Because of these triggers, overthinking sometimes turns into a habit. If you've been overthinking for a long time, your brain has probably become used to this pattern of thinking, and it may take some effort to break the cycle. However, sometimes you don't want to change, or think that you can't, no matter how much you try. After all, overthinking can't be too bad, right? Well, you be the judge. There are a lot of effects that overthinking can have on your mind and body.

The first way that overthinking affects you both mentally and physically is by increasing your stress levels, which has drastic consequences. When you spend too much time dwelling on negative thoughts, it only increases your feeling of nervousness and unease, triggering your body's stress response. This can cause physical symptoms, like increased heart rate, muscle tension, headaches, and even ulcers.

Overthinking can also disrupt your sleep patterns. When your mind is racing with thoughts and worries, it can be difficult to quiet them enough to get a good night's rest. Sleep is incredibly important for our physical and mental health and a lack of sleep has nasty consequences, including irritability, loss of productivity, increased risk of obesity, diabetes, and cardiovascular disease. Sleep deprivation also affects your personal safety, making it more dangerous for you to drive, leading to accidents or injuries.

This combination of consequences can begin to affect every aspect of your life, whether you're a student trying to make it through school or trying to stay focused and motivated during your workday. Overthinking can seriously interfere with the pursuit of your goals in life and interfere with your relationships, leading you to feel lonely or isolated. All of this can ultimately cause you to think negatively about yourself. When you're constantly analyzing and second-guessing your actions, choices and words, it can be easy to fall into a pattern of self-criticism and doubt. This can harm your self-esteem and confidence over time, which may lead to self-sabotaging behaviors.

The longer that you let overthinking cause these symptoms, the worse the cycle of chaos gets. Eventually, you will fall victim to the worst consequence of overthinking, mental clutter. Mental clutter is the term we use to describe the jumbled mess of thoughts, worries, and distractions that can fill your mind and make it hard to focus on anything else, giving you a constant state of low energy, brain fog, and stress. It's like having a cluttered closet – it's hard to find what you're looking for, and the pressure is overwhelming. Your brain gets all foggy and full, and it gets more and more frustrating every time you try to navigate it.

In addition to overthinking, there are a bunch of ways that you can make your mental clutter worse. One common one is a lack of direction in your life. When you're not clear on your goals or priorities, it can be easy to get bogged down by all of the different thoughts and distractions that come your way, especially when you already overthink.

Another way you can contribute to mental clutter is a busy, over-stimulated lifestyle. When you're constantly bombarded by noise, technology and other distractions, your mind gets so loud that it can be deafening. You might find yourself constantly checking your phone or getting lost in social media, even when you know that you should be focusing on other tasks. It feels like your head is literally being weighed down by the clutter of your brain, and you can't do anything else except mindless, immediate activities like playing phone games or endless scrolling.

Another major cause of mental clutter is, wait, I'll give you a moment to guess. Got it? Okay. Stress. Stress is going to be a running theme throughout this book, so get used to it now. Stress is part of a never-ending cycle of overthinking and mental clutter. Overthinking causes stress, which causes mental clutter, which causes more stress. It may seem impossible to escape. When you're under a lot of pressure and dealing with difficult emotions, it's hard to think clearly and focus on anything that truly matters, crippling you into inaction.

Finally, mental clutter can be made worse by lack of self-care. When you're not taking care of your physical and emotional needs, it's difficult to maintain mental clarity and focus. You'll probably be overwhelmed by the simplest task, struggling to entertain the thought of completing it. It's an endless cycle, and it's sometimes unbearable to live that way. So, what do you do about it?

Here's what you're probably thinking:

"Okay, I've sat here and read all of the things that are wrong with me, where it's coming from, and how it's basically making my life a fraction of what it could be. Thanks, now I feel really great."
But wait, the point of this is not to dump all of this on you and say, "good luck buddy." No, you need to know how to fix it!

Where Overthinking Comes From

The first thing you need to do to start to remedy your overthinking is to understand the different factors that lead to overthinking. There are personal factors to overthinking, that is, things that have to do with you individually and that you have at least a little bit of control over. There are also environmental factors, things that happened around you that were outside of your control.

Perfectionism: If you're a perfectionist, you may be more prone to overthinking. You might worry about making mistakes, not meeting your own high standards, or disappointing others. This can lead to over-analyzing situations, which can cause you to get stuck in your own head.

Control Issues: You want to feel like you have some kind of control over the outcome of a situation, and you try to plan and analyze everything to make sure it goes the way you want it to. It's hard to wrap your head around the fact that some things aren't within your control.

Lack of Self-Awareness: If you're not in tune with your own thoughts and emotions, you may find yourself overthinking as a way to try to understand what you're feeling and why you're feeling it. You think that you're soothing yourself when, in actuality, you're making it worse.

Personality: Unfortunately, some people are literally just born this way. Certain personality traits, such as being highly sensitive or introspective, can make you more prone to overthinking. You may have a tendency to dwell on your thoughts and feelings, finding it difficult to let go of negative or worrying thoughts.

Okay, I know you're not feeling better yet, but I promise, this information is important. Outside of personal factors, there are also a few environmental factors that contribute to overthinking.

Past Experiences: This can include trauma but can also be any difficult or embarrassing event that you play over and over again in your mind. You may feel the need to overthink in order to make sense of what happened, like when a high school bully made fun of you for saying a word wrong in your class speech. Again, you think you're making it better, but you aren't.

Social Pressure: The pressure to perform or meet certain expectations can cause you to overthink. This can be especially true in competitive environments, where the stakes are high and there's a lot riding on your performance. Maybe you're on a professional debate team or going to nationals with the volleyball team. These situations can cause anyone to become an overthinker.

Critical Parenting Style: If parents are overly critical or harsh in their feedback, it can lead to feelings of self-doubt and a tendency to overthink things. As a child, you may have been preoccupied with pleasing your parents and avoiding criticism, leading to a cycle of overthinking and anxiety.

Lack of Emotional Support: When the important people in your life aren't supportive, children and even adults can feel isolated and alone in their thoughts and worries. You may have had no one to talk to about your emotions, so your only option was to unload them onto yourself, thinking things through over and over again, trying to gain advice from your own mind.

Overprotectiveness: If parents are overprotective of their children, it can limit their opportunities to learn and grow on their own. You may have been overly dependent on your parents, feeling overwhelmed with every new challenge that you had to face. Because you never learned to resolve these situations on your own, you feel underprepared to solve them, leading you to overthink.

Modeling: At the core, you could have simply grown up around people that constantly modeled overthinking behavior. Parents or guardians who exhibit a tendency to overthink may inadvertently pass it on to others. Children absorb everything they see, learning how to be in the world from their role models. If your role models were overthinkers, it's likely that you are too.

Different Types of Overthinking

Now, not every overthinker is the same. Overthinking can look the same on a bunch of people, but the mental model, or thinking pattern that they use to justify their thinking can be different. It's important to recognize what these patterns are to address them effectively. Let's look at an example of each mental model you could be subscribing to.

Catastrophizing: This is a type of overthinking that involves imagining the worst-case scenario in any given situation. If you're a catastrophizer, (don't ask if that's a real word), you jump to extreme conclusions and become consumed by the "what-ifs" of every situation.

Imagine you're out for a hike with a friend and you take a wrong turn on the trail. As you start to walk back, you begin to catastrophize, imagining all the things that could go wrong. You might think:

"What if we get lost and can't find our way back? What if it gets dark and we have to spend the night in the woods? What if we run out of water and become dehydrated? We could be in serious danger!"

While it's important to take precautions and be prepared for emergencies, it's unnecessary to view a small mistake as an indicator of certain death.

Ruminating: If you overthink using rumination, you replay events or conversations that have happened over and over and over again in your mind until you feel stuck. You're unable to move on from a situation or problem, and it goes unresolved. It's eventually shoved into the closet of mental clutter, building up the pressure and chaos.

Maybe you had an argument with a friend earlier in the day. You keep replaying the conversation repeatedly in your head, thinking about what you should have said or done differently. You think:

"Why did I say that? I should have said this instead. Maybe if I explained myself better, they would have understood. But what if I made things worse by bringing it up in the first place? Maybe I should just apologize and try to move on. But what if they don't want to?"

It is definitely important to reflect on conflicts with people that you love, especially if your ultimate goal is to come to a solution. But this type of thinking may cause the opposite result.

You may never be able to let go of the situation or make amends with someone you've had a disagreement with.

Black and White Reasoning: This is when you look at everything in extreme terms. You're all-or-nothing, 0 or 100, good or bad, right or wrong, you get the idea. You try to fit any situation, even complex ones, into simplistic categories.

You're taking a math test and you get a few questions wrong. You start to think that you're not good at math and you'll never be able to understand it, no matter how much tutoring you get, or practicing you do. You think to yourself:

"I'm just bad at math. I always get questions wrong, and I'll never be able to get it right or understand. I should just give up, accept my failure and focus on other subjects that I'm better at."

Not everything is just good or bad. People can always improve when they put in effort. They may not be as good as a gifted math student, but there is always room to learn. This type of thinking can limit and prevent you from challenging yourself and developing new skills.

Over-Analyzing: This involves trying to find meaning or significance in every detail of a situation or conversation. This will eventually overwhelm you and confuse people as you try to process too much information at the same time.

An exciting day has come: you're buying your first car! You spend hours researching different models, reading reviews and comparing prices. You start to feel overwhelmed and unsure of what to do.

"I've been looking at this for hours and I still can't decide. Maybe I missed something important in the reviews. What if I make the wrong decision and regret it later? I need to keep researching until I'm absolutely sure."

Sometimes there isn't a "perfect" option. You should always make informed decisions, especially ones that are a big commitment. However, indecisiveness and stress shouldn't be a hindrance to making decisions and moving forward with the successes and failures of that choice. Sometimes, there isn't any more information than what you already have.

Perfectionistic Reasoning: Do you set impossibly high standards for yourself, constantly striving for a flawless finish? Maybe you constantly think about all the mistakes you could make, or falling short of your own expectations. If this sounds like you, you're a perfectionist, and you overthink to avoid ever making a mistake.

You're working on a project for school or work. You spend hours making sure every detail is perfect, constantly going back and revising your work, thinking:

"It's not good enough yet. I need to keep working on it until it's perfect. If I don't it won't be good enough and people will think I'm an awful worker. I need to make sure it's right, so I won't be judged for sloppy work."

Striving for excellence is a great quality to have, but it's possible to take it too far. You can easily spiral into burnout, constant self-doubt and anxiety. You lose the ability to accept your progress as you progress to the final destination.

Negative Self-Talking: This is your inner voice that constantly undermines your confidence and self-esteem. Your overthinking comes in the form of constant self-criticism, becoming completely immersed in your own flaws and shortcomings.

Maybe you're getting ready for a fancy social event, but you start to feel self-conscious about your appearance, engaging in negative self-talk:
"I look terrible in this outfit. Everyone is going to notice how bad I look. I'm ugly and unattractive. Why am I even bothering going out?"

This is something that a lot of people experience, even if they aren't overthinkers. But it's especially vicious when you are. It's extremely difficult to enjoy any social situation or leave your house at all, leaving yourself crippled so you can't enjoy a good party or event.

Overthinking can be a common and challenging experience that can impact your mental health and overall well-being. As you've seen, there are so many consequences that you have to deal with when you're an overthinker, getting in the way of what you really want out of life.

It can be caused by a variety of personal factors, past experiences and challenging situations, and it looks different on everyone. You could be a catastrophizer, seeing the doom in every situation, or you could be a negative self-talker, struggling to get rid of that voice in your head that tells you that nothing you do will be enough.

Now that you've received a huge amount of information, it's time to take a pause and reflect. Let's go through what you've learned so far.

Reflection

Are there any personal factors that you think specifically contribute to your overthinking?

_____

_____

_____

_____

_____

Are there any environmental factors that stuck out to you?

_____

_____

_____

_____

_____

What type of overthinker do you think you are? It can be a combination of a few different ones, or just one of them. Which ones resonated with you the most?

_____

_____

_____

_____

_____

The good news is that there are effective strategies and tools that can help you manage and overcome overthinking, which you'll learn about as you keep reading. In the coming chapters we will talk about understanding yourself more fully so you can master the emotions that are the villains behind your overthinking tendencies. You'll understand how to recognize your negative thoughts and transform them into good ones, as well as how to manage your own stress and time. Remember, it's okay to seek help when you're struggling with overthinking. With the right support and tools, you can learn to manage your thoughts and worries more effectively, reaching the goals that you've always wanted to achieve but never felt like you could. So, welcome to the journey; let's get to work!

CHAPTER 2
MASTERING YOUR EMOTIONS

Welcome, my fellow emotional hot mess, to the chapter about mastering your emotions. Ah yes, those pesky things that tend to get the best of us at the worst possible times. Whether you're prone to angry outbursts, uncontrollable tears, or just a general sense of feeling overwhelmed, we've all been there.

But fear not, my friend, for there is hope! By the end of this chapter, you'll be a pro at handling those pesky emotions and preventing them from taking over your life. So, put on your emotional seatbelt, grab some tissues (just in case), and let's get started.

Understanding your emotions can feel overwhelming at first, especially if you're dealing with complex or intense feelings. However, taking the time to truly comprehend your emotions can have a profound impact on your mental-health and overall wellbeing, including overthinking.

One key aspect of learning to understand your emotions is figuring out how to recognize them when they happen. This means paying attention to the physical sensations in your body, thought patterns, and overall mood in reaction to something that happens to you. This will help you identify specific emotions that may be present.

Emotions can have a serious effect on your overthinking behaviors, and it's important to be able to identify your own emotional state. Most people tend to overthink when they are experiencing negative emotions such as anxiety (duh), fear, sadness, or frustration. In these situations, you become preoccupied with past events or potential future outcomes, like you've read in the previous chapter, which will cause you to overanalyze and magnify issues beyond what is necessary. You overthink to cope with your negative emotions because you think it will soothe whatever you're feeling, but it tends to have the opposite effect. Thinking about an issue usually only magnifies your negative emotion; it doesn't diminish it. That's why it's important to understand that overthinking is NOT a good remedy for negative emotions, or positive ones for that matter.

Positive emotions such as happiness and excitement can also lead to overthinking behaviors. In some cases, individuals may become too fixated on exciting, future outcomes, causing them to ruminate excessively about potential scenarios and missing out on the present moment. Even worse, you could picture the perfect scenario for the future in your head due to your excitement and ending up disappointed when that scenario never happens. This puts you into an endless cycle of positive and negative emotions, all of which causes your overthinking to be worse. This is why understanding yourself emotionally is imperative to addressing your overthinking. Let's get into it.

Identifying Your Emotions and Their Meaning

Once you've identified an emotion, it's important to explore it further in order to better understand why you're feeling that way. Seeing words on paper instead of thoughts in your head provides a new perspective; let's start with a framework for exploring your emotions. Choose an emotion that you think often causes you to overthink. This can be anxiety, fear, sadness, frustration, etc.

_____

_____

_____

_____

_____

What usually triggers this feeling? Think of a situation that usually causes you to feel your chosen emotion.

_____

_____

_____

_____

_____

Is this feeling something you can control or influence? If so, how do you usually control or influence your feeling?

_____

_____

_____

_____

_____

This kind of self-reflection can help you gain a deeper insight into your emotional state, identifying the underlying issues that may be contributing to what you feel. Emotions are the underpinnings behind most overthinking, which is why this step is so important. If it's hard for you to do this at first, let's look at some common factors that impact your mood and emotions.

Factors That Impact Your Emotional State

There are a variety of factors that can impact your emotional state on a regular basis; let's start with the physical ones. Can you guess one of the most significant influences? If you guessed sleep, you are right.

Ah, sleep. That elusive, magical, wonderful thing that we all crave but never seem to get enough of. And while we all know that sleep is important for our physical health, did you know that it can also have a major impact on our emotional state? That's right, folks - a good night's sleep can mean the difference between feeling like a superhero and feeling like a cranky toddler who needs a nap.

When we don't get enough sleep, our emotional regulation goes out the window. Suddenly, that little thing that would normally roll off your back becomes the end of the world. You snap at your loved ones, cry over spilled milk (literally), and generally feel like you're on the brink of a meltdown. Not to mention, the irrational thoughts that pop into your head at 3am when you can't sleep just exacerbate your problems. (No, Karen, the world is not actually ending. Go back to sleep.)

Similarly, poor eating habits are another contributor. Listen up, my fellow junk food junky - I hate to break it to you, but that bag of chips you've been munching on is doing more harm than just leaving crumbs all over your couch. Poor eating habits can wreak havoc on your emotional health, leaving you feeling like a soggy piece of lettuce in a sea of fried chicken.

When we fuel our bodies with unhealthy foods, we're basically asking for an emotional rollercoaster ride. One minute you're feeling happy and energized, the next you're crashing harder than a kid coming down from a sugar high. And don't even get me started on the hangry spells - you know, when you're so hungry you could eat your own arm and snap at anyone who crosses your path. (Sorry, not sorry.)

Now, if that's not enough, there's one more villain to your emotional health superhero story: a lack of exercise. Yes, it's true - lounging on the couch all day might feel good at the moment, but it's doing nothing to help your emotional state.

When you don't get enough exercise, you're telling your body and mind to take a vacation from feeling good. Suddenly, you're feeling more stressed, anxious, and just generally down in the dumps. You snap at your loved ones, find yourself crying over the littlest things (like that sappy commercial about puppies), and just can't seem to shake the funk.

The physical stuff is just the tip of the iceberg when it comes to your emotional well-being. Now, let's get into some mental factors. Another significant factor in your emotional well-being is, again, the running theme and arch nemesis of your brain: stress. It's the thing that we all seem to have in abundance, whether we want it or not. It's like that annoying relative that just won't go away, no matter how many times you tell them you're busy. It's like a gremlin that feeds off our happiness and leaves us feeling like a cranky, unfulfilled mess.

When you're stressed, your body and mind go into overdrive. Suddenly, you're feeling more anxious, irritable, and just generally frazzled. You can't seem to focus on anything, your mind is racing a mile a minute, and you're convinced that the world is out to get you. Outside of this, the physical symptoms are almost unbearable - the headaches, the stomachaches, the muscle tension - it's like your body is punishing you for not being able to handle everything all at once.

Stress can manifest in many different ways, to the point where you don't even realize that stress is the thing that's affecting you. Stress can be caused by work pressures, family issues, financial problems, or even everyday inconveniences that build up as you bottle them up. When you are under stress, you feel overwhelmed, exhausted, unable to cope and at serious risk of overthinking, not to mention vulnerable to the host of health problems that are down the road.

So, what do you do with this information? You need to learn how to cope with negative and positive emotions in a healthy way that actually helps you instead of using overthinking as your go-to.

Automatic Negative Thoughts

The first way you can do this is by understanding the necessity of identifying your own thoughts, where they come from and what emotion is guiding them. The most common type of thoughts that will mess with your brain are ANTs. Not the ants that infest a glass of lemonade if you leave it outside for too long; the brain ones. Who doesn't love it when their brain suddenly decides to flood them with a barrage of self-doubt, fear, and negativity for no apparent reason? It's like a little gift from your brain that just keeps on giving - until you feel like crawling into a hole and never coming out, that is. Yes, my friend, automatic negative thoughts are the gift that keeps on giving, and you're lucky enough to have them in abundance.

Automatic negative thoughts (ANTs) are the ones that are typically negative (obviously), repetitive and subconscious. They arise automatically in response to specific situations or emotional triggers, without you actively having to think about them. Common types of ANTs include thoughts that are critical, self-deprecating, and pessimistic, such as "I'm not good enough," "I'll never be able to do this," or "Nothing ever goes my way." These thoughts are so automatic and below your awareness, that you don't even realize that you're bullying yourself. All. Day. Long.

Now, I know what you're thinking: "Well, if I don't know how to recognize negative thoughts, how will I know when I'm thinking negative thoughts?" A confusing question, but here are a few signs that can help you recognize automatic negative thoughts:

Automatic: ANTs tend to pop up without any intentional effort or conscious control. They appear before you even realize what's happening.

Persistent: ANTs stick around, like a family of ants you can't get rid of; it can be difficult to shake off (which is where overthinking comes in). They repeat in your mind and distract you from your goals, causing you to have an overall negative emotional state.

Distorted: ANTs tend to be extreme or exaggerated. They're probably not entirely accurate and may focus on the negative aspects rather than the positive ones. If you find yourself thinking things like "I'm never going to be good at this." It's probably an ANT. The ANT buzz words are "never" and "always." If you're having a thought with one of those words in it, it's probably an ANT.

Another thought prediction: "but if I'm having the thought and I'm feeling negative emotions, won't my emotions get in the way of my realizing that it's an ANT?" This is a good point. Oftentimes, people get so caught up in what they're feeling that it's hard to realize that what you're thinking is automatic, persistent, and distorted. We rarely feel like we're exaggerating when we're feeling badly, which is why when you hear the words, "just relax," it makes you want to do the opposite. Not helpful. So, what can you do?

You have to be deliberate about looking for your ANTs. Looking for automatic negative thoughts is like going on a treasure hunt, but instead of gold and jewels, you're looking for those sneaky little gremlins that are wreaking havoc on your mental state. The good news is that you don't need a map or a compass - just a little bit of self-awareness and a willingness to dive deep into the depths of your own mind. It's kind of like spelunking, but instead of exploring caves, you're exploring the caverns of your own thoughts. So, grab your headlamp, strap on your hiking boots, and get ready to shine a light on those automatic negative thoughts that are hiding in the shadows. You never know what kind of treasure you might find!

Here's where journaling comes in again. It may seem silly to you at first, but it'll seriously help you identify if your thoughts are a serious consideration, or just an ANT trying to mess with your head. Many people have found that keeping an emotional journal is helpful in identifying their negative thoughts and emotions. Let's try it out:

How to Battle Automatic Negative Thoughts

Think of a negative thought that you often have. What words run through your brain? It doesn't have to be a sentence or phrase; it can be a series of individual words. Write whatever comes to mind.

_____

_____

_____

_____

_____

If you said these words out loud to a friend or family member, how do you think they would respond? Would they consider it realistic?

_____

_____

_____

_____

_____

So, you've found yourself face-to-face with an automatic negative thought. Now what? Well, first things first: you need to fact-check that sucker like you're a detective on a mission. Get out your magnifying glass, put on your Sherlock Holmes hat, and start asking questions. Is this thought really true, or am I just being a drama llama? Am I blowing things out of proportion, or is this a legitimate concern? If you're not sure, try doing some research - just make sure you're not falling down a Google rabbit hole of misinformation. And if all else fails, call in the big guns: your best friend, your therapist, your cat (hey, they're great listeners). Sometimes, all you need is a fresh perspective to help you see things in a new light.

Being able to identify an ANT is an amazing step in the right direction, but you can't begin to overcome it if you don't consider the source. ANTs can be influenced by past experiences, beliefs and expectations. It's like playing a game of whack-a-mole - you can keep smacking those pesky thoughts down, but they'll just keep popping up unless you get to the root of the problem. So, start asking yourself questions like: Where did this thought come from? Did someone say something to trigger it? Is it based on a past experience? Sometimes, our automatic negative thoughts can be rooted in deeper issues, like past traumas or insecurities. So, it's important to give yourself the space to explore those underlying causes and work through them. And if all else fails, just blame your parents - it's always their fault anyway, right? Just kidding...kind of.

Again, you may need someone to talk this through with, or use journaling. Oftentimes, writing things down allows you to look at them more objectively.

Where do you think your negative thoughts are coming from? Is it a belief, experience or expectation?

_____

If you decided between the three options above, try to figure out which specific belief, experience, or expectation triggers this thought.

_____

_____

_____

_____

_____

Once you have an awareness of what ANTs are and where they come from, you can start to look for patterns to catch them more efficiently. As you pay attention to your thoughts, try to identify any recurring themes. For example, you might notice that you tend to catastrophize (sound familiar?) when you're running late for an appointment, or you may overgeneralize when something goes wrong. You think that if you're late for the appointment, they won't accept you as a patient, and you would have missed a day of work for nothing (catastrophizing) or that if you do miss the appointment, you're never going to find another doctor who will take you (overgeneralizing). These are tell-tale patterns of ANTs, and recognizing these patterns is extremely important in overcoming them.

Now that you have the tools to recognize your negative thoughts and emotions, let's talk about the strategies you can use to stop ANTs from invading your life and emotions.

Practicing Mindfulness: I'm sure you've heard this before, and you're thinking, "a face mask and a glass of wine is not going to help me stop having negative thoughts. Try again." Contrary to what most people think, mindfulness is a lot more than doing "self-care." Mindfulness includes things that you need to do for your mental health, not necessarily what you want to do. Honestly, mindfulness is hard, and it's a technique that can help you stay present and aware of your own thoughts and feelings without judgment. When you have a negative thought, you have to do the work to observe it without getting caught up in it. That is mindfulness. Introducing another sensation besides your thoughts is a great way to practice mindfulness, bringing yourself back into the present moment instead of getting lost in your deep, dark brain.

Recording what you think and feel, both before and after each of these techniques will allow you to see both your immediate and long-term progress. Trust me, try it out.

One simple way to practice mindfulness is to focus on your breath. Again, this is probably something you've heard before, and it's not going to be a magic cure the first time you try it. But consistency and environment are key. Let's try it now:

What are your current emotions? Write down any words that come to mind.

_____

_____

_____

_____

_____

Find a quiet place to sit or lie down, taking slow, deep breaths. As you breathe, focus on the sensation of the air moving in and out of your body. If your mind starts to wander, gently bring your attention back to your breath.

Do you feel any different? If so, in what ways?

_____

_____

_____

_____

_____

Again, you have to remain consistent, practicing this a number of times before you start to see a result. If you don't want to do this exercise now, you can always do it during a situation when you are overthinking and feeling anxious, and record what happens. Nothing good comes easy, and it's important to put in the work and show up for yourself.

Now, let's talk about body scanning. No, not the kind of body scanning where you get patted down by TSA at the airport - we're talking about a mindfulness technique that involves scanning your body from head to toe, checking in with each part of your body and noticing any sensations or tension you might be holding onto. It's like giving yourself a full-body massage, minus the weird spa music and cucumber water. So, find a comfortable position (no need to contort yourself into a pretzel), close your eyes, and start at the top of your head. Take deep breaths in and out, and as you exhale, release any tension you might be holding in your forehead, temples, and jaw. Move down to your neck and shoulders, and notice any tightness or soreness you might be feeling. As you exhale, imagine that tension melting away like butter on a hot biscuit. Keep scanning down your body, taking deep breaths and releasing any tension you might be holding. It's like playing a game of "Operation" with your own body - but instead of trying to remove a rubber band from inside a tiny plastic guy, you're trying to let go of any physical or emotional stress you might be carrying. And if you accidentally hit the buzzer and the nose lights up, don't worry - nobody's perfect, and it's all part of the process.

Mindful eating is a lesser-known technique for practicing mindfulness. This kind of eating involves paying attention to the taste, texture and experience of eating a food. When you're overthinking, try this exercise.

What emotions are you feeling?

_____

_____

_____

_____

_____

Take a small piece of a food you like, such as a raisin or a piece of chocolate, and examine it closely. What is the color, texture, and smell of the food in your hand?

_____

_____

_____

_____

_____

Take a small bite, savoring the taste and texture as you chew slowly. You may feel super weird when you do this the first time, and that's okay. Keep focused on the fact that everything you're doing is for your health. What does it taste like? What describing words can you think of?

_____

_____

_____

_____

_____

As you continue to eat, pay attention to how full you're feeling. Are you still hungry, or are you starting to feel satisfied? It's like playing a game of "Hunger Detective" - but instead of solving a crime, you're tuning in to your own body's signals. Try to eat slowly and mindfully, paying attention to your body's signals of fullness. This can help you avoid overeating or feeling uncomfortable after a meal.

_____

_____

_____

_____

_____

_____

_____

This is another reason why having the right environment is absolutely necessary when completing these techniques. You need to feel safe and secure to try new things. If you're trying to do these in front of a bunch of people, you're probably going to struggle.

The last mindfulness technique is mindful exercise. This involves paying attention to your surroundings and the experience of walking, or doing any physical activity that you enjoy. As you complete this exercise, focus on the sensations in your body, such as the movement of your legs or the feeling of your feet on the ground. If possible, try to do your exercise outside; that way you can pay attention to your surroundings, noticing any sights, sounds or smells.

Remember, practicing mindfulness is about being present and aware in the moment. Try to approach these exercises with a sense of curiosity and openness, without judging your thoughts or experiences. With time and practice, mindfulness can help you feel calmer and more centered in your daily life.

Practicing Positive Self-Talk: I know, another one you've probably heard before, but these techniques are popular for a reason. These things need to be done right to be effective, and oftentimes they aren't. People want these exercises to work the first time they try it, and unfortunately, that's not the case. No one expects to go to the gym, do one workout, and have a body builder physique the very next day. They don't go and yell at their trainer demanding a refund because they didn't have results overnight. The same thing goes for your mental health.

To practice positive self-talk, focus on positive, affirming statements that support your well-being. This is yet another instance where keeping a journal would be extremely helpful. For example, if you record in your journal that you're feeling anxious, as you write down the ANT that is taking over, you can write under it: "I am capable of handling stressful situations." Positive self-talk comes in a variety of ways, and you can use different ones for different situations. Let's try it out.

The first is affirmations. These are positive statements that build self-confidence, like what you would say to a friend if they're feeling down. Choose a few affirmations that resonate with you, such as "I am worthy of love and respect." Repeat these affirmations to yourself regularly or write them on sticky notes and put them on the mirrors in your house. These can be extremely helpful when you're feeling down or overwhelmed.

Think of a common ANT that pops into your mind during a stressful situation or experience. Write it down here.

_____

_____

_____

How can you turn it into a positive affirmation? Think of a way you can flip the thought to make it positive. Write the affirmation here.

_____

_____

_____

The next technique for positive self-talk is reframing. This involves looking at a situation from a different perspective. It's a little harder to do when you're in the midst of a negative thought, but you can master it with practice. For example, if you are stressed before a public speaking event, you might reframe your thought from "I'm going to mess up and embarrass myself," to "I'm prepared and capable of doing a good job." Now, personalize it for yourself.

If you're feeling anxious about an upcoming event, like a presentation at work or a speech you have to give, what might you think to yourself?

_____

_____

_____

Picture yourself as a friend who is hearing you say your negative thoughts out loud. How would they respond? Write down your answer, trying to reframe the negative thought.

_____

_____

_____

Congratulations, you've reframed a negative thought!

Gratitude is a very important part of positive self-talk, and one that people miss frequently. The warm, fuzzy feeling you get when you realize that life isn't all doom and gloom. But let's be real - when you're in a funk, it can be hard to feel grateful for anything. That's where practicing gratitude comes in. Think of it like exercising your gratitude muscle. It's like doing bicep curls, but instead of weights, you're lifting thankfulness.

Take a few minutes to reflect on what you're grateful for. Focus on the things you like about your city, job, friends and family. Maybe try to think of things you're grateful for that you often overlook. Maybe you're grateful for the cup of coffee you have every morning, or the music you listen to on the way to work or school. Write whatever you think of.

_____

_____

_____

_____

_____

_____

_____

_____

As you go about your day, make a mental note of things you're grateful for. Did someone hold the door open for you? Did you see a pretty flower on your walk to work? Did you finally catch that one green light on your commute? It doesn't have to be anything grandiose, just something that made you feel good.

_____

_____

_____

_____

_____

_____

_____

_____

Focusing on the good in your life can help you feel more positive and optimistic, having the tools to battle negative thoughts more aggressively. You can also keep a gratitude journal to help cultivate your gratitude practice. Write down three things you're grateful for each day - it can be as simple as "I'm grateful for my fuzzy socks" or as profound as "I'm grateful for my loved ones' health and happiness." Just don't write "I'm grateful for my collection of antique spoons" every day, because that's just weird.

The last self-talk technique is visualization. Again, if you're an artistic soul, this one is definitely for you. Close your eyes and imagine this: you're on a beach, sipping a piña colada, and basking in the warm sun. You can feel the sand between your toes and the ocean breeze on your face. Ah, doesn't that feel nice?

That, my friend, is the power of visualization. It's like a mini mental vacation where you get to create your own happy place. And the best part? You don't need a passport or to even leave your couch to do it.

To get started, think about a situation or outcome you'd like to manifest in your life. Maybe you're trying to land your dream job or work up the courage to ask out your crush. Whatever it is, close your eyes and picture yourself achieving that goal. Imagine all the details - the sights, the sounds, the smells, the feels. Let yourself feel the excitement and joy of having that desire fulfilled.

Visualization is like a dress rehearsal for your dreams. It helps you get into the mindset of already having what you want, which can boost your confidence and motivation. Plus, it's a fun way to spend a few minutes in your own imagination.

If you're feeling skeptical, just remember that some of the most successful athletes and entrepreneurs swear by visualization. They use it to mentally prepare for big events and envision their success. So, the next time you're feeling stuck or anxious, close your eyes and take a mental trip to your happy place. It might just be the boost you need to make your dreams a reality.

If you're feeling up to it, you can even draw what that might look like. For example, if you're nervous about a job interview, imagine yourself walking into the interview room feeling calm and confident, answering all the questions with ease.

Remember, all of this takes a lot of practice. Be patient with yourself and approach these techniques with an open mind. Sometimes, they may not work for you immediately, and that's okay. You're making strides toward better health, which is amazing!

Surrounding Yourself with the Right People: You know what they say: you're the average of the five people you spend the most time with. So, if you're constantly hanging out with negative Nancys and Debbie downers, it's no wonder you're feeling a little down in the dumps.

But fear not! You have the power to curate your own squad of positive, supportive people who uplift and inspire you. Think about the people in your life who make you feel happy, motivated, and energized. These are the folks you want to surround yourself with.

Of course, we can't always choose who we have to interact with (hello, annoying coworker or family member). But you can control how much time and energy you give to those relationships. Focus on nurturing the connections that make you feel good, and don't be afraid to set boundaries with those who bring you down.

Identifying your values is the first step in figuring out if you have the right people in your life. Take some time to think about your values, and write what's important to you in your relationships. Do you value honesty, kindness, loyalty, or something else? When you know what you're looking for in your relationships, it can help you identify the people who are a good fit for you, and who may not be.

_____

_____

_____

_____

_____

_____

_____

_____

_____

_____

Setting boundaries is another must in creating healthy relationships. Be clear about what you're comfortable with and what you're not. If someone is consistently negative or draining, it's okay to limit your time with them or cut them out altogether. Now, this is easier said than done, because ending any type of relationship is difficult. However, you should always be your first priority, and sometimes that means making hard decisions.

If you've found that you've cut a lot of negative people out of your life, you might be starting over with your friend group. That's okay! It's time to seek out positive influences. Look for people who uplift and inspire you whenever you talk to them. Seek out friends, mentors or role models who have qualities or accomplishments that you admire. Surrounding yourself with positive influences can help you feel more motivated and inspired. In turn, you can uplift and inspire them!

If you want good friends, you have to be a good friend. Active listening is a skill that can help you build stronger, better relationships. When you're having a conversation with someone, it's important to give them your full attention and do your absolute best to understand their perspective. Ask open-ended questions and show empathy and understanding. Modeling what you want out of a friendship is a good way to draw positive people into your life.

Another good tactic for a beneficial social life is joining groups or activities. If you're reading this as an introvert, I just felt you cringe. But seriously, joining a group or activity that aligns with your interests can be a great way to meet new people who share your values and passions. This isn't to say that you have to show up to a knitting party next week, but you can start with a social media group and go from there. Whether it's a volunteer group, a sports team, or a book club, finding a community of like-minded people can help you feel more connected and supported in pursuing a better lifestyle for yourself. Be patient and persistent in your search for positive relationships, and don't be afraid to let go of ones that no longer serve you.

Stopping negative thoughts takes time and practice. Be kind to yourself as you navigate the practices of mindfulness, positive self-talk, and surrounding yourself with the right people. All of these things take a lot of work and consistency, and it won't come easily. But, if you find the right things and people to get you going, you'll look back at yourself and be shocked about who you've become.

Confronting Trauma

Now, we've covered how to navigate those pesky ANTs, but why do we even start having them in the first place? The answer is simple: trauma. Past experiences shape us into who we are, and that includes our emotional wellbeing. We can grow up with a wonderful wellbeing, free of any intrusive, ridiculous, and negative thoughts, or we can experience things in life that make it harder for us to navigate our emotions. Practicing all the techniques you've just read will eventually lead you to the source of your thoughts and feelings, which is the past.

It's hard to let go of what's happened, especially if it was something that altered your life forever. Overthinking is a classic method of dealing with the negative emotions that come with past experiences, and you'll never get over them if you can't let go of the past. When you're not held back by old regrets or painful memories, you have more space to focus on your personal growth and development. Dwelling on the past can interfere with every good thing you've just read about. It can strain your relationships with others, your ability to handle future challenges, and hinder mindfulness. Being weighed down by the past keeps you from fully engaging with the world around you, restraining you from experiencing greater joy and fulfillment in your daily life. If you don't overcome this, you won't overcome your emotional struggles or overthinking. So, let's get into how to do this.

Practice Self-Compassion: Look, let's face it: life can be tough. And sometimes, we go through some seriously traumatic stuff that can leave us feeling like we're stuck in a never-ending spiral of despair. But here's the thing: you don't have to go through it alone.

One of the most important things you can do for yourself when you've experienced trauma is to practice self-compassion. This means treating yourself with the same kindness and understanding you would offer to a close friend or family member who was going through a tough time.

Instead of beating yourself up for how you're feeling or how you're coping (or not coping), try to approach yourself with empathy and understanding. Recognize that what you've been through is hard, and it's okay to feel however you're feeling.

Give yourself permission to take things at your own pace and to ask for help when you need it. And remember: healing is not a linear process. You might have good days and bad days, and that's completely normal.

By showing yourself some self-compassion, you can begin to heal from your trauma and move forward in a more positive and hopeful direction. So go ahead and give yourself a hug (or a virtual hug, if that's more your style). You deserve it.

Write down what you regret about the past, or any mistakes you wish you could undo. Then, write down what a friend would say if they were forgiving you for them.

_____

_____

_____

_____

_____

_____

_____

_____

_____

_____

_____

_____

Change Your Perspective: So, you've had some pretty tough experiences. Maybe you've gone through a traumatic event, or maybe you've faced ongoing challenges that have left their mark on you. It's understandable that you might see these experiences in a negative light, and feel like they've permanently messed you up. But what if I told you that you can change your perspective on trauma and actually come out stronger?

First, let's acknowledge that trauma is a real thing, and it's not something to take lightly. But what if we started to see trauma as a teacher, rather than a destroyer? What if we viewed our difficult experiences as opportunities to learn and grow, instead of things that hold us back? Changing your perspective on trauma can take time and effort, but it can be done. One way to start is by reframing your thoughts. Instead of thinking, "I'm so messed up because of what happened to me," try thinking, "I've been through some tough stuff, but it's made me who I am today, and I'm pretty darn resilient because of it." See what I did there? It's all about flipping the script and focusing on the positive.

Try answering these questions as a way to work through changing your perspective on your trauma:

"What lessons can I take from these experiences?"

_____

_____

_____

_____

_____

_____

_____

"How have they shaped me into the person I am today?"

_____

_____

_____

_____

_____

_____

Reframing your perspective can help you feel more empowered about what has happened, and what positive outcomes are possible.

Forgive Others: Forgiveness can be a powerful tool for letting go of the past. This doesn't mean you have to forget what happened or condone harmful behavior, but it can mean releasing any bitterness you hold in your heart and welcoming acceptance. Forgiveness is hard, especially when someone has caused you pain or trauma. It's natural to want to hold onto your anger and resentment, and maybe even seek revenge. But what if I told you that forgiveness is actually for you, not for the person who hurt you?

When you hold onto anger and resentment, it eats away at you like a bag of stale Cheetos. It doesn't do anything to the person who hurt you, but it sure does a number on your own emotional well-being. That's why forgiving someone, even if they don't deserve it, is one of the most powerful things you can do for yourself.

Now, let me be clear: forgiveness doesn't mean excusing or justifying what someone did to you. It doesn't mean you have to forget what happened or pretend like it didn't hurt. It simply means letting go of the anger and resentment you're holding onto and moving forward.

Forgiveness can be a long and difficult process, but it starts with a decision. You have to decide that you're ready to let go of the anger and resentment, and that you're willing to work on forgiving the person who hurt you. From there, it's all about taking small steps, like practicing empathy and compassion, or focusing on the positive things in your life.

Remember, forgiveness is a gift you give to yourself. So go ahead, take a deep breath, and let go of that stale bag of Cheetos. Your emotional well-being will thank you for it. Take a moment to write down the names of people you need to forgive in your life. If you don't feel safe to do that, make up some aliases that only you would know.

_____

_____

_____

_____

_____

Focus on the Present: This is where mindfulness comes in. You already have the techniques, and it's great to use them towards focusing on the present instead of the past. When you find yourself ruminating on past events, try to bring your attention back to the present moment. Focus on your breath, your surroundings, or any physical sensations you're experiencing. Some people even say that it's helpful to them to state their name, age, birthday, and where they are currently; "I'm in my car" for example. This can help you feel centered and grounded in the present.

Seek Support: Letting go of the past can be a difficult process, and it's okay to seek support from friends, family or a therapist. Talking through your feelings with someone you trust can help you gain perspective and feel more supported. If you trust them enough, they can even gently push you towards the forgiveness that you need in your life. Write down the names of some people in your life that you trust to support you.

_____

_____

_____

_____

_____

Letting go of the past is a journey, and it's okay to take it one step at a time. Be patient with yourself as you work through your feelings, and trust that you have the strength and resilience to move forward.

When you are in control of your emotions, you are better equipped to manage overthinking. Firstly, you're less reactive. When you're in control of your emotions, you're less likely to react impulsively to your thoughts and feelings. Instead, you're able to respond thoughtfully and rationally, which can help to reduce overthinking. Secondly, you're more self-aware. When you're aware of your emotions and how they affect your behaviors, you can recognize when you are starting to overthink things. Third, you can regulate your thoughts. This can help you to stop overthinking by redirecting your thoughts to more positive or productive topics. Lastly, you can better manage stress, which, as we know, is a big dog in overthinking. Overall, being in control of your emotions is an important aspect in managing overthinking.

In conclusion, mastering your emotions is not an easy feat, but it is certainly worth the effort. By making small changes in your daily habits, such as getting enough sleep, exercising regularly, eating healthy, and practicing mindfulness, you can drastically improve your emotional well-being. By recognizing automatic negative thoughts and taking steps to challenge them, you can break free from limiting beliefs and patterns that are holding you back.

It's also important to surround yourself with positive and supportive people, and to practice self-compassion and forgiveness, especially when it comes to dealing with past traumas. Remember, you are in control of your emotions, and you have the power to shape your own narrative and perspective.

So go ahead, take charge of your emotional state, and don't be afraid to seek help if you need it. With practice and patience, you can become the master of your emotions and lead a happier, more fulfilling life.

CHAPTER 3
CHANGING NEGATIVE THOUGHTS INTO POSITIVE ONES

We all have negative thoughts from time to time. Whether it's self-doubt, fear, or worries about the future, negative thoughts -as we learned in the previous chapter- can hold you back and make you feel stuck. However, the good news is that we already learned to recognize them, and in this chapter, learn how to replace them with positive ones. As you read, you'll explore practical strategies for replacing negative thoughts and cultivating a more positive mindset.

Cognitive Distortions

Cognitive distortions are patterns of thinking that are irrational, unhelpful, and often inaccurate; basically, take the 'distorted' part of ANTs and turn it into its own evil mind alien. I know they seem very similar, but let's spend a minute talking about how they're different.

So, cognitive distortions are like the magician's assistant, distracting you from the truth with their illusions and misdirections. They take a grain of truth and twist it into something completely different, like a game of telephone gone wrong. You start with "I made a mistake," and suddenly it becomes "I'm a complete failure who can't do anything right and will never succeed in life." Talk about a dramatic transformation!

On the other hand, automatic negative thoughts are like a broken record player, playing the same sad song over and over again. They're those pesky little voices in your head that tell you all the bad things that could happen or how terrible you are, without any real evidence to back it up. It's like your brain is stuck on the pessimistic channel, and you can't change the station.

So, in summary, cognitive distortions are like a magic show that tricks you into believing something that isn't true, while automatic negative thoughts are like a never-ending sad song that you can't turn off. Both can be pretty annoying, but with a little humor and some cognitive-behavioral therapy, you can learn to see through the illusions and change the tune!

Understanding cognitive distortions is an essential step in learning how to manage your brain effectively, because cognitive distortions destroy your view of reality. The most common kind of cognitive distortion is jumping to conclusions. Yes, everyone does this, but with cognitive distortions, it's like if you jumped to conclusions with moon shoes on. Remember those? If you don't, Google it; I promise you won't be disappointed.

Another reason why cognitive distortions are so nasty is because your brain tells you that everything is your fault, rooted in a shred of information. It's like being the star of your own personal soap opera, where every little thing that happens is somehow a reflection of your worth as a person. But let's take a playful look at this distortion, shall we?

Imagine you're walking down the street, and someone you know walks right by you without saying hello. If you're prone to personalization, you might think, "Oh no, they must be mad at me! I must have done something wrong!" But let's play a little game of "What if?"

What if they're just in a rush to get somewhere and didn't notice you?

What if they're preoccupied with something else and didn't register your presence?

What if they're having a bad day and it has nothing to do with you?

See how many different scenarios there could be? Personalization is like putting on a pair of blinders that only let you see things from your own perspective. But when you start to play "What if?" and consider other possibilities, you open yourself up to a wider range of interpretations. The possibilities are endless, and it probably isn't you. But, it's really hard to convince someone with cognitive distortions that these thoughts are, in fact, distortions. This is because they also have a strong hold on your emotional reasoning.

Emotional reasoning is when you assume that your emotions reflect reality, which is usually not the case. For example, if you feel anxious about an upcoming presentation, you might assume it's because you're not prepared even though you spent hours getting ready. With cognitive distortions, your emotions guide your logical reasoning instead of the other way around. It's impossible for you to see the positives, causing you to minimize them and maximize the negatives.

This makes it harder for you to receive feedback with any type of constructive criticism, as you'll only see it as an offense against who you are, not the work that you did. On the opposite end, you'll dismiss any positive feedback as no big deal, thinking that the person who complimented you is just trying to be nice to soften the blow of the negatives. Cognitive distortions completely wreck your view of reality and make your brain a big pool of self-deprecating thoughts. This is why it's important to learn some strategies to manage them.

You should already be implementing mindfulness, positive self-talk and seeking support. These three things will make a huge difference in your cognitive distortions. You should be continuing to write down any thoughts that make you feel icky inside, because identifying negative thoughts is the first step in learning how to stop them. Like you've already read, once you can recognize cognitive distortions, you can begin implementing the right steps to combat them.

How to Fight Cognitive Distortions

The first step to battle cognitive distortions is thought-stopping. When you notice a negative thought and feel the spiral of sadness start to form in your stomach, you need a quick cue to snap you out of it. This is especially useful if you're in a space where you aren't able to immediately practice the other techniques for which you need a quiet, safe space. Come up with either a physical or verbal cue to stop the thought in its tracks. For some people, they might say "stop!" out loud, but others think that's too awkward and uncomfortable. Other people make a gentle pinch on their wrist or arm in order to be less noticeable. Over time, your brain will begin to associate this stimulus with "oh wait, I'm not allowed to think that."

Another playful way to use thought-stopping is to imagine your negative thoughts as annoying salespeople trying to sell you something you don't want. When they start their sales pitch, you can say, "Sorry, not interested!" or "No, thank you!" and imagine them walking away with their tail between their legs.

The key to thought-stopping is to catch the negative thought early and replace it with a more positive or realistic one. It takes practice, but the more you do it, the easier it becomes. So, next time you catch yourself spiraling into negative thinking, try hitting the "pause" button and changing the station. Who knows, you might even start to enjoy the new positive tune playing in your mind!

Again, this is a quick and proactive way to stop any cognitive distortions, and you should be combining this with other strategies. Some of the most useful ones to combat overthinking are commonly used in Cognitive Behavioral Therapy.

We've talked about seeking support, and one type of support that people often avoid is therapy. Somehow, therapy turned into a dirty word that only exists for people with real problems; that's a cognitive distortion by the way. Therapy is a tool that is necessary for a lot of people, and you shouldn't be afraid of using it to help you. Cognitive Behavioral Therapy (CBT) is a type of therapy that focuses on changing negative thoughts, beliefs and behaviors that contribute to psychological distress, with overthinking included. It's a widely used, well-established treatment and can be helpful for a variety of problems.

Cognitive Behavioral Therapy

CBT's core principle is that our thoughts, feelings and behaviors are all interconnected, which is exactly what you've been reading about so far. Our thoughts influence our emotions, and our emotions influence our behaviors. More specifically, our negative thoughts make us feel anxious and stressed, and our stress causes us to overthink in an effort to make ourselves feel better. It works the other way around too, which is where the cycle of overthinking comes from. Stress causes overthinking, and overthinking causes more stress.

In CBT, the therapist and client work collaboratively to identify and challenge negative thoughts and beliefs that contribute to stress. The therapist helps the client develop strategies that replace negative thoughts and beliefs with more realistic, positive ones. These strategies may involve cognitive restructuring and behavioral experiments, which basically helps you to both reframe a negative thought and test different ways of behaving in real-life situations.

CBT also emphasizes the importance of learning and practicing new skills to manage symptoms of distress. It provides a tailored, personalized opportunity for people to address their overthinking in specific situations that uses a structured and time-limited treatment. Typically, CBT involves a set number of sessions, ranging from 12-20 on average. This makes it an effective and efficient treatment for many people. Although you are learning so many tools and resources by reading this book, it's important to have someone to help you with specific overthinking situations in which you find yourself.

Besides thought-stopping, CBT employs tons of other strategies to help people overcome their problems with overthinking. It will make the most sense to explain them from easiest to hardest, so let's start with the easiest.

Thought Challenging: Oh sure, thought challenging, because who doesn't love a good mental workout? It's like playing a game of "Stump the Brain" - except this time, you're the one doing the stumping!

So, let's say you have a negative thought, like "I'm never going to find a job." You can challenge that thought by asking yourself, "Is that really true, or am I just being a drama queen?" And then you can come up with alternative thoughts that are more positive or realistic, like "Maybe I haven't found the right job yet, but that doesn't mean I won't in the future."
It's like a mental game of "Whose Line Is It Anyway?" where everything is made up and the points don't matter. But in this case, the points are your mental health and well-being, so they actually do matter.

Of course, thought challenging takes practice, so don't worry if you're not an expert at it right away. It's like going to the mental gym - you have to build up those mental muscles. But with time and practice, you'll be able to catch those negative thoughts and challenge them like a pro. And who knows, maybe you'll even start to enjoy the mental workout!
By examining the evidence and questioning your assumptions, you can start to shift your perspective and reduce overthinking. Let's try it.

Think of a recent situation that triggered negative or distorted thinking for you. Write down the negative thought that came to mind, and then ask yourself the following questions:
Is this thought based on fact, or just my interpretation of the situation?

_____

_____

_____

_____

_____

What evidence do I have to support this thought?

_____

_____

_____

_____

_____

_____

_____

_____

Are there alternative explanations or interpretations of this situation that are more realistic or positive?

_____

_____

_____

_____

_____

_____

_____

_____

_____

_____

Next, try to come up with at least two alternative thoughts or perspectives that challenge the negative or distorted thought. Write down each alternative thought and consider how it might change your emotional response to the situation.

_____

_____

_____

_____

_____

_____

_____

_____

_____

_____

Finally, reflect on how you felt during the process of thought challenging. Did it help you gain a more balanced perspective on the situation? Did it reduce the intensity of your negative emotions? Write down your thoughts and any insights you gained from this exercise.

_____

_____

_____

Remember, thought challenging takes practice, so don't worry if you don't come up with the perfect response right away. The important thing is to keep challenging your negative thoughts and beliefs to build more realistic and positive thinking patterns over time.

Cognitive Restructuring: This involves identifying the underlying beliefs and assumptions that are driving your overthinking, and then working on replacing those unhelpful beliefs with more positive and accurate ones. This is reframing, and it's important that you have a trusted individual in your corner to help you through specific instances where you need to reframe your thoughts. This is also something you already have some background information about, so it should be less of a challenge for you to complete this technique. Either way, it's important to keep practicing!

Let's use the same negative thought from the thought challenging exercise. Try to restructure the negative thought or belief by creating a more positive and realistic statement. For example, if your negative belief is "I'm not good enough", you could restructure it to "I have strengths and weaknesses, and I'm constantly learning and growing."

Write down your new statement and consider how it might change your behavior or emotions in situations where you would normally have negative thoughts or beliefs.

_____

_____

_____

_____

_____

_____

_____

_____

Finally, reflect on how you felt during the process of cognitive restructuring. Did it help you to gain a more positive and realistic perspective on the situation? Did it reduce the intensity of your negative emotions? Write down your thoughts and any insights you gained from this exercise.

_____

_____

_____

_____

_____

_____

_____

_____

_____

_____

_____

Remember, cognitive restructuring takes time and practice, so don't expect to see immediate changes. But with consistent effort, you can gradually shift your negative thinking patterns and improve your overall well-being. Let's get into the more nuanced techniques that you haven't heard yet.

Self-Scripting: This is an amazing exercise that is used in CBT and one that you can do right now. It involves creating a written script or dialogue that reflects the way you would like to think or behave in a particular situation. For example, if you struggle with social anxiety and tend to feel nervous or self-conscious in social situations, you might create a self-script that includes positive and reassuring statements. But this is more than just a positive affirmation. You need to create a movie script that includes all those affirmations. No Post-It Notes, but rather an actual storyline in which the plotline is focused on the situation you're overthinking about.

By writing out these statements in a real-life scenario, and practicing them regularly, you can start to rewire your thought patterns and build more positive beliefs about yourself and your abilities. Self-scripting can be a powerful tool for anyone looking to overcome cognitive distortions and achieve their goals, and you're no different. Try thinking of a situation that you often overthink about. Write out that situation and include positive affirmations that will make the situation less stressful for you.

_____

_____

_____

_____

How do you feel after doing this exercise?

_____

_____

_____

_____

Now we're going to get into the more complicated techniques, ones that are going to be a challenge and require you to do things that you really don't want to do.

Behavioral Activation: This involves finding ways to engage in enjoyable or meaningful activities, even if you don't feel like it at first. This can help to break the cycle of overthinking, as you'll be focusing your attention on something positive instead of ruminating on negative thoughts. There are four key principles of behavioral activation that are important to understand if you want to do this correctly:

1. Start small. When you're feeling overwhelmed by overthinking, you can find it hard to imagine doing anything positive or rewarding. That's why it's important to set achievable goals. For example, you might start by taking a short walk outside, or doing a simple activity that you used to enjoy, such as doodling. Write down a small activity that can be a possible go-to for behavioral activation.

_____

_____

_____

_____

2. Schedule it. One of the key elements of behavioral activation is scheduling your activities in advance. This can help to ensure that you have a plan in place, and can help you avoid getting stuck in a rut. Try to schedule a mix of activities that you enjoy and that challenge you in a positive way. It may even be helpful to download a scheduling template online, and fill it in with an overthinking situation, and the activity you're going to do to counteract it.

3. Focus on values. Behavioral activation is not just about doing things that feel good in the moment. It's also about connecting with your values and doing things that are meaningful to you. For example, if you value creativity, you might try taking an art class or starting a new project with a new art material you haven't tried yet. Take a second and write down three values that you think are important in your activities.

_____

_____

_____

_____

4. Keep track of your progress. It's an amazing thing when you're able to pull yourself out of overthinking with an activity, and it's even better when you're able to reflect on how the experience made you feel. This can help you to see progress over time, giving you a sense of accomplishment and motivation to keep going during the times where you don't want to.

Behavioral activation is another technique that will take time and determination. However, by taking small steps towards positive activities and connecting with your values, you can start to break out of your negative cycles. Let's move onto the hardest technique to master in CBT.

Exposure Therapy: This involves gradually exposing yourself to situations or stimuli that trigger your overthinking, in a controlled and safe way. Let's say that you're someone who tends to overthink social interactions and worry about what others think of you. You might avoid anything social or spend a lot of time contemplating the negative interactions you've had in the past. To address this pattern of overthinking, there are some steps to take if you want to try exposure therapy.

The first step of exposure therapy usually involves identifying a specific social situation that triggers you. For example, it might be attending a party where you don't know many people. Identify one now.

_____

_____

_____

_____

Next, you need to create a hierarchy of exposure tasks. This will most likely involve gradually exposing yourself to increasingly challenging social situations, starting with something relatively easy like making small talk with a stranger at a coffee shop, working your way up to attending that large party mentioned in the first step. This list should be created with someone who is a licensed therapist that has an understanding of what you would mentally be able to handle as you work up to your situation.

As you work your way up through the hierarchy, you will need to use the coping strategies that you've been learning about so far. This would include breathing, self-talk, body scans, or even mindful eating. You need these to help manage your anxiety and overthinking as you challenge yourself with these tasks. The goal is to help you learn that you can handle these situations without getting overwhelmed by anxiety or caught up in negative thoughts.

It is highly recommended that you have a good understanding of the techniques you have learned so far, having a full understanding of which ones help you the most and what you can turn to in times of stress and anxiety. You cannot complete exposure therapy with the absence of the coping skills that counteract negative thoughts. It's also highly recommended that you complete exposure therapy with a licensed therapist. Having the support and guidance of a qualified professional can help ensure that what you're doing is safe, effective and tailored to your individual needs.

Now, let's talk about your options if an actual therapist isn't open to you. You can still complete all these exercises on your own; it will just take more time and practice. If you follow these techniques and stay consistent, it can only go up from here. Include a trusted friend or family member to read over your journal entries and tell you what they think; it may help you gain some insight. So, if therapy isn't an option for you, no big deal. But how can you find restructuring, positive thoughts if you don't have anyone to bounce ideas off of?

How to Find Positive Thoughts

It's important to know that finding positive thoughts is not about denying or ignoring negative feelings or experiences. Rather, it's about learning to see situations in a more balanced and accurate way, building a more positive and resilient mindset. So where can you start? Here are some different types of positive thoughts that you can turn to in order to replace the negative ones.

The Opposite Thought: The easiest way to challenge a negative thought is to write down the exact opposite. For example, what's the opposite of "I'm not good enough?" "I am good enough." This is a small, baby step towards reframing negative thoughts that is simple to think of. Once you can do this, you can move on to more complex ideas.

Negative thought: _____

Opposite thought: _____

The Problem and Solution Thought: Another, more complex way to restructure negative thoughts is to look at it as a problem that requires a solution. If you're thinking to yourself "I'll never be good enough at this," a solution can be "I can do hard things, and I can improve over time." This is a little bit trickier to accomplish, but you can do hard things and improve over time. See? I just did it. This makes you ponder what attributes you do have in order to solve the problem that your brain is pressing onto you.

What's the problem?

_____

_____

_____

What's the solution?

_____

_____

_____

The Hopeful Thought: After you've mastered the previous two kinds of positive thoughts, you can move into a more ambiguous type of thinking: hopeful thoughts. Believe in the possibility of positive outcomes and keep an optimistic attitude. This will not be easy in the beginning, but you can challenge yourself to write down even the smallest piece of optimism to battle a negative idea. You probably need to ask yourself leading questions. For example, when you think "I'm not good enough," write down an answer to the question: "what am I good at?" Having the foundation of the opposite thought acts as the foundation for you to think of possible 'opposites' to a situation. Think of it outside of the subject area, situation, or experience that caused you to think of the initial, negative statement. You can try to do this now to get some practice.

Negative thought:

_____

_____

Hopeful thought:

_____

_____

Finding Gratitude: This is by far the hardest kind of positive thinking to master, and you will need consistent practice with the other three to prepare you for finding gratitude. This will be a more automatic ability for you as time goes on, and you'll be able to focus on the good things in your life and express gratitude for them. This will shift your focus from what you lack to what you have and promote feelings of contentment. Identify steps you can take to move towards your goals and take action towards them wherever you can. Even small steps can help build momentum and create a sense of progress and accomplishment. Gratitude allows you to appreciate the positive over the negatives, which is what you're working towards. You can start by writing down five things that you're grateful for at the beginning of the week or day. This can be as simple as a warm cup of tea, a kind gesture from a friend or a beautiful sunset.

5 things you are grateful for:

1. _____

2. _____

3. _____

4. _____

5. _____

You can also find gratitude by expressing it to others. Take the time to express your gratitude to people in your life who have made a difference. Write a thank-you note, send a text or email, or simply tell them in person how much you appreciate them. Visual reminders are also useful to give yourself an attitude of gratitude. Place reminders of the things you're grateful for around your home or workspace. This could be a picture of a loved one, a quote that inspires you, or a small trinket that holds special meaning. Remember, practicing gratitude is a powerful way to cultivate your mindset, and it's the final step to positive thinking.

Cognitive behavioral therapy can be a highly effective treatment for overthinking. By helping individuals identify and challenge negative thought patterns, CBT can help reduce your anxiety, depression and other symptoms of overthinking. Replacing negative thoughts with positive ones is a powerful technique that shifts your focus away from the negative, and it's a major step towards overcoming overthinking. By consciously choosing to reframe the cognitive distortions that invade your brain and showing them in a more positive light, you can begin to change how you think in every way, including how you think about yourself and the world around you.

While all of this can seem very challenging and overwhelming, it's important to see everything you do as you read this book as small steps towards progress. You can read as much or as little as you need, and stop whenever you think you're overwhelmed. That's the beauty of a book; you can tell it to shut up whenever you want. If you commit to the process, you can learn to break free from this cycle. So, let's keep going in small steps, slaying one overthinking villain at a time.

Well folks, if you're feeling overwhelmed by your cognitive distortions, fear not! You have a whole arsenal of tools at your disposal to battle those pesky negative thoughts.

First up, we have thought stopping - because who doesn't love interrupting their own train of thought every five seconds? It's like playing a game of mental whack-a-mole!

Then we have cognitive restructuring, where you get to play mind games with yourself and try to convince your brain that things aren't actually as bad as you thought. It's like trying to persuade a stubborn toddler that vegetables are actually delicious. Good luck with that!

Next up, we have behavioral activation - where you force yourself to do things you don't really want to do in order to feel better. It's like a never-ending game of mental tug-of-war, but with yourself as the rope.

And let's not forget about self-scripting, where you get to write your own version of reality like some kind of wannabe author. Who needs real life when you can just make up a better one in your head?

And finally, we have exposure therapy - where you confront your fears head-on and hope for the best. It's like playing a game of mental chicken with yourself. Fun!

In all seriousness though, battling cognitive distortions can be a tough and ongoing process. But with time, patience, and the right tools, you can learn to manage your negative thoughts and live a happier, more fulfilling life. So, get out there and start whacking those moles! Or, you know, whatever other technique works best for you.

CHAPTER 4
LEARNING TO DE-STRESS

Welcome to another chapter of your new favorite book. Today, we're going to talk about something that's near and dear to our hearts, and something that really gets us overthinkers all riled up: stress!

Let's face it, stress is just a fact of life. We all experience it at some point or another, whether it's due to work, relationships, or just the state of the world. And when you're an overthinker, stress can feel like a never-ending nightmare that just won't go away.

But don't you worry, because there are some things you can do to help manage that stress, keeping your mental and physical health in check. We're going to explore some tried and true methods for de-stressing and finding some dang peace.

You already know about mindfulness, you know, that fancy term for paying attention to the present moment without judgment. But wait, there's more! We'll also delve into the world of aromatherapy, journaling, spending time in nature, and other all-powerful tools for reducing stress and finding some peace of mind. And of course, we'll throw in some stress-busting prompts for good measure.

So let's get to it. By the end of this chapter, you'll have some new tools in your belt for managing stress and keeping those overthinking tendencies at bay. Because when it comes to stress, the key is to find what works for you and make it a part of your regular routine. You got this!

Let's start with some short, easy ways to lower your stress:

De-Stressing Techniques

Listen to Music: Now, I know what you're thinking. How can listening to music possibly help with stress? Well, my friend, the science is in, and the data doesn't lie. Studies have shown that listening to music can have a significant impact on reducing stress and anxiety levels.

In fact, a study conducted by the University of Nevada found that listening to music can reduce stress levels by up to 41%! That's right, just by putting on some tunes, you could be reducing your stress levels by almost half. And who doesn't love a good dance party to relieve some tension?

But it's not just about the numbers. Listening to music can also have a profound emotional impact on our mood and well-being. It can bring us comfort, inspire us, and help us to connect with our emotions in a healthy way. So, whether you're listening to a relaxing playlist or jamming out to your favorite songs, music can be a powerful tool in managing stress.

So, the next time you're feeling overwhelmed, try putting on some of your favorite tunes and see how it makes you feel. Trust me, your mind and body will thank you for it.

Create a playlist of songs that make you feel happy and relaxed, and listen to it when you're feeling stressed. Think of 10 songs that would work for this right now and write them down.

1. _____

2. _____

3. _____

4. _____

5. _____

6. _____

7. _____

8. _____

9. _____

10. _____

Get Organized: Sometimes feeling stressed is simply a result of feeling overwhelmed by everything that you feel you have to do. According to a survey conducted by the National Association of Productivity and Organizing Professionals, 82% of respondents reported that being organized had a positive impact on their stress levels. And it's not hard to see why. When our spaces are clutter-free and well-organized, we're better able to focus, prioritize tasks, and feel a sense of control over our environment.

But it's not just about physical organization. Mental organization is just as important in reducing stress. When our thoughts are scattered and disorganized, it can be hard to focus and feel in control. That's where tools like to-do lists, calendars, and journaling can come in handy. By taking the time to organize our thoughts and tasks, we can reduce stress and feel more confident in our ability to tackle whatever comes our way.

So, whether it's decluttering your space or organizing your thoughts, taking steps towards being more organized can have a significant impact on reducing stress levels. Give it a try and see how it makes you feel. Trust me, you'll thank yourself for it later.

Laugh: I know, this one sounds silly. But laughter is a powerful stress-buster, so try to find ways to inject some humor into your day. They say laughter is the best medicine, and when it comes to stress, that couldn't be more true. There's just something about a good belly laugh that can instantly relieve tension and make us feel better. But what's the science behind this? Let's take a closer look.

Studies have shown that laughter can have a significant impact on reducing stress and anxiety levels. In fact, a study conducted by Loma Linda University found that laughter can lower cortisol levels, which is a hormone associated with stress. Not only that, but laughter can also increase the production of endorphins, which are our body's natural feel-good chemicals.
But it's not just about the physical benefits. Laughter can also have a profound emotional impact on our well-being. It can bring us closer to others, help us to connect with our emotions, and provide a much-needed break from the stresses of everyday life

So, how can you incorporate more laughter into your life? There are plenty of ways! You can watch a funny movie, read a humorous book, or even just spend time with friends who make you laugh. Whatever it is, make sure to take the time to laugh and enjoy the moment.
In conclusion, laughter is a powerful tool in reducing stress levels. So, don't be afraid to let loose and have a good laugh. Who knows, it may just be the best thing you do for your mental and physical health today.

Everyone is different, so it's important to find what works for you when it comes to de-stressing. Don't be afraid to try new things and see what helps you relax and feel more centered. That's exactly why we're going to keep going through different techniques. You don't have to do them all, but it's important to at least try them and see what works. So let's keep trucking along.

We already know about mindfulness, but we also got exercise. I can hear you now: "yeah, we already covered mindful exercise." But, that's not what we're talking about here. We're talking purposeful, consistent exercise that can be an amazing tool to use in handling stress. I know, I know, sometimes just the thought of exercise can be stressful in itself. But hear me out - moving your body releases endorphins, those feel-good chemicals that can help lift your mood and ease stress.

Whether it's a brisk walk, some gentle yoga, or a hardcore workout, make it part of your regular routine. When exercise is something that you really don't want to do, you won't make it a habit. But there isn't one way to exercise, or two, or three. There are hundreds of options for consistent exercising, and surely you can find one you enjoy. There's kayaking, rock climbing, weightlifting, running, swimming, tennis the list goes on and on. Maybe you don't know which exercise you like, and that's okay! Let's start by writing down 5 ways that you can move your body that you want to try.

1. _____

2. _____

3. _____

4. _____

5. _____

And don't forget about the power of group exercise. Joining a fitness class or sports league can not only help you get your sweat on, but it can also provide a sense of community and social support. Plus, it can be a great way to try something new and step out of your comfort zone. Now, I know what some of you might be thinking. "I just don't have time to exercise!" And I get it; life can be busy - but here's the thing, exercise doesn't have to take up a lot of time. Even just 10-15 minutes of movement each day can make a difference.

So, whether you're a seasoned gym-goer or a complete exercise newbie, find what works for you and make it a regular part of your routine. Your body and mind will thank you for it! Try each of those 5 exercises and record what you liked and didn't like about it. Write about whether you think it's something you could do every day, or a few times a week, etc.

_____

_____

_____

_____

_____

_____

_____

_____

_____

_____

_____

_____

_____

_____

_____

_____

Okay, so we got exercise down. What else? Let's not forget about the power of a good old-fashioned hobby. Doing something you enjoy can be a great way to take your mind off of your worries and get lost in the moment. Whether it's painting, gardening, playing music, find something that brings you joy and make time for it regularly. Again, if you don't know where to start, write some down that you want to try.

1. _____

2. _____

3. _____

4. _____

5. _____

Hobbies can be a fantastic way to reduce stress and take your mind off of overthinking. Not only can hobbies be a great stress-reliever, they can also provide a sense of accomplishment and purpose. When you're working on a project or pursuing a passion, you're tapping into your creativity and building skills that can be incredibly rewarding.

When it comes to relieving stress, we all have our go-to methods. Maybe it's binge-watching Netflix, taking a long bubble bath, or indulging in some comfort food. That's right, those hobbies you love doing in your free time can also double as stress-relieving techniques.

For example, a study conducted by the *American Journal of Public Health* found that engaging in creative hobbies, such as painting or knitting, can reduce the levels of cortisol, a hormone associated with stress. Not only that, but engaging in a hobby you enjoy can also help to distract your mind from the stresses of daily life and provide a sense of accomplishment.

But it's not just about creative hobbies. Physical hobbies, such as hiking or dancing, can also be effective in reducing stress levels. In fact, research has shown that exercise can release endorphins, which are our body's natural mood-boosters.

So, whether it's picking up a new hobby or diving deeper into an existing one, taking the time to engage in an activity you enjoy can have a significant impact on reducing stress levels. So, next time you're feeling overwhelmed, why not try your hand at something new? Who knows, it may just become your new go-to stress-relieving technique.

And let's not forget about the social aspect of hobbies. I know, if you're an introvert you can just ignore me. Joining a group or club centered around your hobby can provide a sense of community and connection with others who share your interests. Plus, it can be a great way to learn new things and get inspiration for your own projects.

I know, I know. Again, we run into the time issue. I'm not unrealistic; I know you have a life to live that includes a lot of other things that demand your time besides a hobby. But hobbies can also be something that you work on for 10-15 minutes a day. Dedicating small amounts of time every day working towards something is worth a lot more than taking a single day over the course of a year to practice your painting, even if it's an entire day.

Do the same thing with hobbies as you did with exercise. Every time you try a new hobby, write about the experience here.

_____

_____

_____

_____

_____

_____

_____

_____

_____

_____

_____

_____

_____

_____

_____

_____

Okay, now that we've added some more things to your plate to de-stress (I know, it seems backwards), let's talk about something that basically takes no time at all: aromatherapy. This is a technique that uses essential oils to promote relaxation and reduce stress.

Essential oils are derived from plants and contain the natural fragrances and properties of the plant. When inhaled or applied topically, they can have a range of therapeutic effects on the body and mind. Some essential oils that are commonly used for stress relief include lavender, chamomile, bergamot, and ylang-ylang. These oils have been shown to have calming and soothing properties, helping to reduce feelings of anxiety and tension.

One way to use essential oils for aromatherapy is to add a few drops to a diffuser or humidifier. This can create a relaxing and calming environment in your home or workspace. Another way to use essential oils is to apply them topically. You can add a few drops to a carrier oil, such as coconut or jojoba oil, and use the mixture as a massage oil or body lotion. Or, you can add a few drops to a warm bath and soak for a relaxing and rejuvenating experience.

Now, it's important to note that not all essential oils are safe for everyone. Some oils can cause skin irritation or allergic reactions, and some should be avoided during pregnancy or if you have certain health conditions. So, it's important to do your research and consult with a healthcare provider or trained aromatherapist before using essential oils.

But if you do choose to incorporate aromatherapy into your stress-relief routine, it can be a wonderful way to promote relaxation and reduce overthinking. So, grab some lavender oil and let's get to relaxing!

Now, you should only use these techniques once you've already covered self-care and mindfulness. They're the foundation that you'll be building all of these techniques on top of. Don't forget what you've already learned; use them along with these techniques.

Another technique to try, which you should know by now is a good one, is journaling. Writing down your thoughts and feelings can be a great way to get them out of your head and onto paper. Plus, it can help you identify patterns in your thinking and give you insight about how your mind works. We've already said this before, but it's important to remind you of its benefits.

One of the great things about journaling is there are no rules or restrictions. You can write about anything you want, in any way that feels comfortable to you. Some people like to write in a stream-of-consciousness style, while others prefer to make lists or jot down specific thoughts or events from their day. While the prompted journal entries here are an amazing start, journaling on your own will only add to the value you're getting from this.

Journaling helps you identify patterns or triggers that may be contributing to your stress or overthinking. By looking back at what you've written, you may start to notice certain themes or recurring thoughts that you can work on addressing. And let's not forget about the therapeutic benefits of writing in general. Research has shown that writing about emotional experiences can have a range of positive effects, including improved mood, reduced symptoms of anxiety and depression, and even improved immune function.

So, whether you prefer to write in a notebook or use a digital journaling app, consider making journaling a regular part of your stress-relief routine. It's an extremely useful way to help understand your own mind, which is why you're writing straight into this book. But, the blank lines in here can only take you so far. Having a journal allows you to extend and duplicate the prompts that are included in here, so you can use them over and over again for a variety of situations. It can be a simple yet powerful way to take care of your mental health; get yourself some fancy writing utensils and get to work!

Grounding Techniques

One of the main skills that you can master in order to de-stress is using grounding techniques. These are similar to the mindfulness techniques that you learned in Chapter 2, but they have a different end goal in mind. So, if they sound familiar, you can try them in a different way to de-stress.

Breathing Exercises: You know how to do breathing exercises, but breathing to reduce stress is different from breathing to reduce anxiety or overthinking. By taking deep breaths and exhaling slowly, you can calm down your nervous system to reduce stress. The main one to use is the 4-7-8 method. This involves inhaling for 4 seconds, holding your breath for 7 seconds, and exhaling for 8 seconds. This exercise is easy to do and can be done anywhere, from the comfort of your own home to a busy office.

Progressive Muscle Relaxation: This is a grounding technique that involves tensing and relaxing different muscle groups in your body. It can help you release physical tension and promote relaxation.

To practice PMR, you typically start by finding a quiet and comfortable place to sit or lie down. You begin by tensing a specific muscle group, such as your foot or hand, and hold the tension for a few seconds. You then release the tension and allow the muscle group to relax completely for another few seconds. Then, you would move onto the next muscle group, working your way up your body until you have tensed and relaxed every portion of your body.

There are many different muscle groups that you can focus on during PMR, such as your hands, arms, shoulders, neck, jaw, stomach, back, buttocks, and legs. Some people prefer to work through each muscle group systematically, while others prefer to focus on specific areas of tension or discomfort. For example, many people feel pain in the shoulder as a result of stress. That can be a muscle group to pay attention to.

While you work through each muscle group, it's important to focus on the physical sensations of tension and relaxation. You might notice a feeling of warmth or heaviness as you relax each muscle group. It's also important to focus on your breaths, taking slow, deep ones as you release tension and relax your muscles.

Guided Imagery: This involves listening to a guided meditation or visualization that takes you through a specific experience or journey. This technique can help you relax and reduce stress by taking you to a calm and peaceful mental space.

To practice guided imagery, you typically start by finding a quiet and comfortable place (as usual). Close your eyes and focus on your breath. Once you are relaxed, begin to imagine a specific scene or scenario that is calming and peaceful to you.

The scene that you imagine can be anything that makes you feel calm and relaxed, such as a beach, forest, meadow or mountain. You might imagine the sound of the waves crashing on the shore, the smell of the fresh mountain air, or the feel of the sun on your skin.

As you visualize this scene, you engage all of your senses to make the experience more vivid and immersive. You might imagine the colors of the sunset, the texture of the sand between your toes, or the taste of the salty air. The more detailed and vivid your visualization, the more effective it can be at promoting relaxation and reducing stress.

Guided imagery can be practiced alone or with the guidance of a trained professional, such as a therapist or meditation teacher. There are also many guided imagery scripts and recordings available online that you can use to guide your practice. Try it on your own and record your experience. Try to engage all of your senses and describe something for each one in your vision (sight, smell, touch, taste and sound).

_____

_____

_____

_____

_____

_____

_____

_____

_____

_____

_____

_____

_____

_____

_____

_____

_____

_____

_____

_____

_____

_____

_____

_____

_____

_____

_____

_____

_____

Grounding Objects: Some people find it helpful to carry or wear grounding objects, such as a piece of jewelry or small stone, that they can touch or hold when feeling overwhelmed. This technique can provide a sense of comfort and stability in stressful situations.

These objects can be anything that has special significance or meaning to you, such as a piece of jewelry, a small stone or crystal, a favorite photograph, or a special trinket. The object should be small enough to carry with you and discreet enough to use in public if needed.

When you are feeling overwhelmed or disconnected you can use your grounding object to help you feel more present and grounded in the moment. Grounding objects can be particularly helpful during stressful or triggering situations, such as public speaking, flying on a plane, or attending a social event. You might hold the object in your hand, touch it, or simply keep it in your pocket. The act of touching or holding the grounding object can help you focus on your senses and bring you back to the present. You might notice the texture of the object, the weight of it in your hand, or the way it catches the light. By focusing on these sensory details, you can calm your mind and reduce feelings of anxiety and stress.

Try to think of something that you have right now that you can use as a grounding object. It should be something that carries significant importance to you.

_____

_____

So to sum it up, de-stressing using these different techniques can be the magic wand that you need to combat the anxiety-inducing effects of overthinking. As we've seen, practices such as deep breathing, progressive muscle relaxation, guided imagery, and grounding objects are all ways to help us stay present and stop the mind from running off like a crazy horse. You don't have to be mindfulness gurus to benefit from these techniques; we just need to be open to trying them out. Because let's face it, we all need a little help managing our crazy thoughts and feelings.

With these techniques in our toolbox, we can find our way back to a sense of calm and control. In the immortal words of Tina Fey, "You can't be that kid standing at the top of the water slide, overthinking it. You have to go down the chute." So, let's get down that chute and embrace the power of de-stressing techniques to give yourself a better life.

Now, I know it seems like all of this information will only bring you more stress. You're probably thinking to yourself, "how am I going to find the time to implement all these techniques?" I get it, feeling like you don't have enough time for everything is a major source of stress, and it's important to know how to feel less pressed for time. This is why in the next chapter, we're going to do a deep dive into time management, a mountain you must climb if you are hoping to stop overthinking. See you on the next page.

CHAPTER 5
MANAGING YOUR TIME

We've all been there - it's 2 AM and your mind is racing with all the things you need to get done tomorrow, next week, or even next year. Your thoughts are spiraling out of control, and before you know it, you're overwhelmed and unable to sleep. It's a vicious cycle, but there's a solution - time management

Yes, I know, time management sounds boring and like something only your overly organized friend would care about. But trust me, it's a game-changer when it comes to reducing overthinking and stress.

When you take the time to plan out your day, week, or even month, you give yourself a roadmap to follow. Instead of worrying about all the things you need to do, you can focus on one task at a time and feel a sense of accomplishment as you check them off your list.
But it's not just about productivity. Time management can also give you a sense of control over your life. By prioritizing your tasks and setting realistic goals, you can avoid the feeling of being overwhelmed and stressed.

So, the next time you find yourself overthinking and stressing about all the things you need to do, take a step back and consider implementing some time management strategies. Who knows, it may just be the solution you need to finally get a good night's sleep. Before we get into the strategies, you need to understand the huge role that time management has in your life, especially in relation to control, procrastination and prioritization, self-care and reducing feelings of being overwhelmed.

The Role of Time Management in Overthinking

First is control. When you feel like you're at the mercy of your schedule and to-do list, it's not a big leap for you to start feeling helpless and overwhelmed. When it comes to overthinking, control is often the root cause of our anxieties. We want to control every little thing in our lives, from the big decisions to the smallest details, and when we can't, our minds go into overdrive.

It's like trying to control a rollercoaster - you can grip onto the safety bar and scream all you want, but in the end, you're still at the mercy of the twists and turns.

But here's the thing - control is just an illusion. No matter how hard we try, we can't control everything in our lives. And that's okay! In fact, it's liberating when you realize that you don't have to have everything figured out.

Remember: you can't control the weather, but you can control how many umbrellas you own. So go ahead and buy that rainbow-colored umbrella you've been eyeing - it won't solve all your problems, but at least it'll brighten up a rainy day.

Secondly, time management reduces procrastination. This one is more of an obvious one, but it's a major source of stress for many people. When you put off tasks until the last minute, you're more likely to feel rushed and stressed out as the deadline for it looms over your head like a big, dark cloud. We all do it, whether we're putting off doing laundry or avoiding that big work project. But here's the thing - procrastination is a major cause of overthinking and stress.

When we procrastinate, we create a backlog of tasks that we know we need to do, but haven't yet tackled. And as that list grows longer and longer, our minds start to race with all the things we need to do, creating a vicious cycle of overthinking and stress.

But fear not! There is a solution, and it's a simple one - time management. When you break down your to-do list into manageable chunks and schedule out when you'll tackle each task, you'll find that you're much more productive and less likely to fall into the procrastination trap.

Third, time management will help you prioritize. Ah, priorities - we all have them, whether it's finishing that work project or binge-watching the latest Netflix series. But when it comes to overthinking, a lack of prioritization can be a major culprit.

When we don't prioritize our tasks, we end up with a jumbled mess of things we need to do, want to do, and maybe shouldn't be doing at all. And as we try to juggle all of these competing demands, our minds start to race, wondering what we should tackle first, and whether we'll have enough time to get everything done.

Time management is here to save the day once again! By taking the time to prioritize your tasks, you can avoid the overthinking and stress that comes with a cluttered to-do list.

And let's be real - who doesn't love crossing things off a to-do list? When you prioritize your tasks and use time management techniques to tackle them one by one, you'll find that you're much more productive and efficient, which means more time for the things you actually want to do.

Fourth, time management gives you more time for self-care. You heard about all the fun, creative things you can do to reduce your stress in the previous chapter, but I'm sure you're wondering where the heck you're going to find the time to do all that. Taking care of ourselves is essential for our mental and physical well-being, but when we're caught up in the endless cycle of overthinking, self-care can often fall by the wayside.

Whether it's taking a long bath, going for a walk in nature, or just curling up with a good book, self-care activities give us a chance to recharge and unwind. And when we're feeling more relaxed and refreshed, we're better able to tackle the challenges of our day-to-day lives, including overthinking.

But here's the thing - self-care isn't something that just happens. We have to make time for it, and that's where time management comes in. By using our time more effectively and prioritizing our tasks, we can actually create more space in our schedules for self-care activities.

So, the next time you're feeling stressed and overwhelmed by your to-do list, take a step back and think about how you can make time for self-care. Whether it's by delegating some tasks, using time management techniques to be more efficient, or just saying "no" to some commitments, remember that self-care is essential for your well-being. And when you take care of yourself, you'll be better equipped to tackle whatever challenges come your way - including overthinking.

I know, we haven't solved the "time" part yet, but just keep reading, we're getting there. It's so important for you to understand the benefits before you see the strategies. It helps you see why you should be doing what you're doing instead of blindly following the commands of a book, which is just weird.

Finally, time management will make you less overwhelmed. Your to-do list, I'm sure, can feel absolutely never-ending. But isn't feeling overwhelmed the same as feeling stressed? What's the difference? Let's get into a quick little vocab lesson.

Stress and being overwhelmed are related but distinct experiences. Stress is a response to a challenging or demanding situation, such as a work deadline or difficult conversation with a friend. Stress can actually be good in small doses; it can motivate you to take action and get things done. However, too much stress can also be harmful and lead to physical and emotional exhaustion. With stress, it's all about balance.

Being overwhelmed, on the other hand, is a feeling of being completely swamped or buried by the demands of your life. It's that feeling of having too much to do and not enough time to do it. A variety of factors can cause the feeling of being overwhelmed including work, family, or personal obligations. It can be hard to shake off and it can leave you feeling depleted and burnt out.

So, while stress and feeling overwhelmed can both be tough to deal with, it's important to recognize the difference between the two. Stress is often an immediate response to a specific situation, while being overwhelmed is a more general feeling of being burned out. You have to manage both, but in different ways.

Feeling overwhelmed is a common trigger for overthinking. When we have too much on our plate, it's easy to feel like we're drowning in a sea of responsibilities and to-dos. But with effective time management, we can combat this feeling and reduce overthinking.

One of the key benefits of time management is that it allows us to break down our tasks into smaller, more manageable pieces, which you're about to learn how to do. When we have a clear plan for what we need to do and when we need to do it, it's easier to focus on one task at a time, rather than feeling like we have a million things hanging over our heads.

By breaking down our tasks into smaller chunks, we can also prioritize more effectively. See, it's all connected! We can identify the tasks that are most important or time-sensitive and tackle those first, rather than getting bogged down in less urgent tasks that may not be as important.

Now that we've explored the impact of time management on overthinking, let's dive into some techniques that can help you manage your time effectively. By setting clear goals, prioritizing tasks, creating a schedule, breaking tasks into smaller steps, limiting distractions, and being flexible, you can reduce stress and feeling overwhelmed, and minimize overthinking.

These techniques are not one-size-fits-all, and what works best for one person may not work as well for another. However, by trying out different strategies and finding what works best for you, you can develop a system that helps you manage your time more effectively, reduce stress, and combat overthinking. So, let's get started!

Setting Clear Goals

Setting clear goals is a crucial step in effective time management. When we have a clear idea of what we want to achieve, we're more likely to stay focused, be productive, and minimize overthinking.

But don't just take my word for it – research supports the importance of goal-setting. In one study, participants who wrote down their goals were significantly more likely to achieve them than those who didn't. Another study found that people who set specific, challenging goals were more motivated and performed better than those who set vague or easy goals.

So, what does it mean to set clear goals? It means taking the time to think about what you want to achieve and why. It means breaking down those larger goals into smaller, more manageable pieces, so you have a clear path forward. And it means setting specific, measurable, and time-bound targets so that you can track your progress and stay motivated.

Without clear goals, it's easy to get lost in the shuffle of day-to-day tasks, to feel overwhelmed, and to succumb to overthinking. But by taking the time to set clear goals, you can stay focused, motivated, and on track. So, let's brainstorm some goals, and start putting your time management skills to work!

Think about a specific goal you'd like to achieve over the next few months. It could be related to your work, personal life, health, or any other area that's important to you. Write it clearly and specifically. What do you want to achieve, and what steps will you need to take to get there?

_____

_____

_____

_____

Next, ask yourself why this goal is important to you. What will achieving it help you accomplish or feel? How will it improve your life?

_____

_____

_____

_____

Think about any obstacles or challenges you might face along the way. What are some potential roadblocks?

_____

_____

_____

_____

Now that we've talked about the importance of setting clear goals, it's time to discuss how to prioritize your tasks to ensure that you're making progress towards those goals. Prioritization is an essential time management skill that can help you minimize stress, maximize productivity, and reduce overthinking.

Prioritizing Tasks

Managing time is the bane of every procrastinator's existence. But fear not, my friends! Prioritizing your tasks is a key element in effective time management, and it's not as daunting as it may seem.

When we prioritize our tasks, we're essentially deciding which tasks are most important and need to be completed first. This allows us to focus our energy on the tasks that will make the biggest impact and minimize the stress that comes with trying to do everything at once Studies have shown that prioritizing tasks can increase productivity and reduce stress levels. A study published in the Journal of Educational Psychology found that individuals who prioritize their tasks reported lower levels of stress and higher levels of productivity compared to those who didn't prioritize.

So, don't let your to-do list overwhelm you. Take some time to prioritize your tasks and enjoy the sweet relief of being in control of your time!

When it comes to managing your time, not all tasks are created equal. Some tasks are more important or urgent than others, so it's important to prioritize accordingly. Try using the "Eisenhower Matrix" to categorize your tasks into four quadrants:

- Important and urgent
- Important but not urgent
- Urgent but not important
- Neither important nor urgent

This can help you determine which tasks require your immediate attention and what can be postponed or delegated. But, what's the difference between important and urgent?

Important tasks are those that have a significant impact on your long-term goals, values, or well-being. These are the tasks that align with our priorities, and that we feel are meaningful or fulfilling. Examples of important tasks might include spending time with loved ones, working on a long-term project, or exercising regularly to maintain good health.

Urgent tasks, on the other hand, are those that require immediate attention or action. These tasks often have a deadline or a sense of urgency attached to them, and they may be related to unexpected events or emergencies. Examples of urgent tasks might include responding to an urgent email, attending to a sick family member, or fixing a broken appliance.

The difference between important and urgent tasks is that urgent tasks demand immediate attention, while important tasks may not have an immediate deadline but are still crucial for long-term success and happiness. It's easy to get caught up in the urgency of tasks and neglect important ones that don't have an immediate deadline. However, it's important to remember that prioritizing important tasks can have a significant impact on our long-term goals.

So, let's practice prioritization. Start by reflecting on your current approach to prioritizing tasks. Do you often find yourself getting caught up in urgent, but unimportant tasks? Are there important tasks that you've been neglecting because they don't have an immediate deadline?

_____

_____

_____

_____

_____

_____

_____

_____

_____

_____

_____

Think about your goals and values. How can you use the Eisenhower Matrix to ensure that you're focusing on tasks that align with these goals and values?

_____

_____

_____

_____

_____

Use the Eisenhower Matrix to categorize your tasks based on their level of importance and urgency.

Important and urgent:

_____

_____

_____

_____

_____

Important but not urgent:

_____

_____

_____

_____

_____

Urgent but not important:

_____

_____

_____

_____

_____

Not urgent and not important:

_____

_____

_____

_____

_____

Finally, reflect on how the Matrix helped you prioritize your tasks. What insight have you gained about your priorities and values, if any?

_____

_____

_____

_____

_____

The Eisenhower Matrix is the trusty method we all know and love. But if you're not loving it, there are other techniques that work just as well.

One such technique is the "Eat That Frog" method, which was made popular by Brian Tracy's book of the same name. The concept is simple – you tackle your most difficult or unpleasant task first thing in the morning, thus "eating the frog" and freeing up your mental energy for the rest of the day.

Research has shown that this method can be effective in reducing procrastination and increasing productivity. A study published in the *Journal of Business Research* found that individuals who completed their most difficult task first reported lower levels of procrastination and higher levels of job satisfaction.

Write down a list of tasks that you've been putting off for a while.

_____

_____

_____

_____

_____

Write down one task that you've been avoiding.

_____

_____

Next, write down three reasons why this task is important and needs to be done.

_____

_____

_____

_____

_____

_____

_____

_____

Write down the first small step that you need to take to get started on the task.

_____

_____

_____

_____

_____

Schedule a specific time in your calendar for when you'll work on this task. Check this box when you've done it!

☐

Finally, reflect on any obstacles that might get in the way of completing this task and brainstorm ways to overcome them.

_____

_____

_____

_____

_____

_____

_____

_____

_____

_____

Remember, the key to the Eat the Frog method is to tackle the task that you've been avoiding first thing in the morning, so that you can free up mental space and have a more productive day. Good luck!

Another method is the "ABCDE" method, which involves analyzing your tasks in a series of questions, which we'll try out now.

Write down a list of tasks that you need to complete. You can use the same one from the "Eat the Frog" technique. Next to each task, write down the consequences (A) of completing or not completing the task. Think about the short-term and long-term consequences of each task.

_____

_____

_____

_____

_____

_____

_____

_____

_____

_____

_____

_____

_____

_____

_____

_____

Write down your beliefs or thoughts (B) about each task. What makes a task important or unimportant to you? What is your current attitude towards each task?

_____

_____

_____

_____

_____

_____

_____

_____

_____

_____

_____

_____

_____

_____

_____

_____

_____

_____

_____

_____

Identify any emotional responses (C) that you have towards each task. Do you feel motivated or discouraged? Excited or overwhelmed?

_____

_____

_____

_____

_____

_____

_____

_____

_____

_____

_____

_____

_____

_____

_____

_____

Rank each task in order of priority (D) based on the consequences, beliefs, and emotions associated with it.

_____

_____

_____

_____

_____

_____

_____

_____

_____

_____

Finally, create a plan of action (E) for completing the tasks in order of priority. Consider any challenges that may arise and how you can overcome them.

_____

_____

_____

_____

_____

_____

_____

_____

_____

_____

So, whether you prefer to "eat the frog" or use the "ABCDE" method, the key is finding a prioritizing technique that works best for you and sticking to it. Who knows, you may just become a productivity machine!

Congratulations on prioritizing your tasks! Now that you have a clear understanding of what needs to be done, it's time to create a schedule to help you manage your time effectively.

Creating a Schedule

The ultimate guide to being an adult. But in all seriousness, creating a schedule is a crucial step in managing your time effectively.

Not only does it help you stay organized and on track, but it also reduces stress and anxiety that come with uncertainty and chaos. Research has shown that creating a schedule can lead to better time management and productivity, as well as improved overall well-being.

One study published in the *Journal of Occupational Health Psychology* found that employees who had control over their work schedules reported lower levels of burnout and job stress. Another study published in the *Journal of Educational Psychology* found that students who had a more structured schedule performed better academically and reported less stress.

So, if you're feeling overwhelmed and disorganized, it might be time to give scheduling a try. Trust me, your future self will thank you.

Once you have a clear goal in mind, it's time to create a schedule. Whether you prefer to use a paper planner, a digital calendar, or a combination of both, creating a schedule can help you visualize how you'll spend your time and ensure that you're making progress towards your goals. Try to be realistic when creating your schedule, building in breaks and downtime to avoid burnout.

There are a few different scheduling techniques that you could use. Not every technique works for everyone, so try a few of them out until you find what works for you! We're going to talk about the pros and cons of all of them.

Time blocking - Time blocking is a popular scheduling technique that many people use to manage their time effectively. The idea is to divide your day into chunks of time, and assign specific tasks or activities to each block.

One of the benefits of time blocking is that it helps you stay focused and avoid distractions. When you have a set time for each task, you're less likely to get sidetracked by other things that come up throughout the day. Plus, it can help you prioritize your tasks and ensure that you're making progress on your most important projects.

However, time blocking can also have its drawbacks. For one, it can be difficult to estimate how long certain tasks will take, and unexpected issues can throw off your entire schedule. Additionally, some people may feel overwhelmed or stressed by having such a structured day Despite these challenges, there is some evidence to suggest that time blocking can be an effective way to manage your time. In a study published in the *Journal of Experimental Psychology*, researchers found that participants who planned out their days using time blocks were more productive and less stressed than those who didn't.

Ultimately, whether or not time blocking is right for you will depend on your personal preferences and work style.

Pomodoro technique – To practice the Polodoro Technique, you work for 25-minute intervals; you break up the intervals with five-minute breaks. After four intervals, you take a longer 15-30 minute break. The technique has positives and negatives.

On the plus side, the Pomodoro Technique is great for people who struggle with procrastination or have trouble focusing for long periods of time. It breaks your work into manageable, 25-minute intervals, which can make it feel less overwhelming. Plus, the frequent breaks can help you stay fresh and engaged throughout your workday.

There's also some evidence to suggest that the Pomodoro Technique can improve productivity. One study found that employees who used the technique completed tasks faster and had better quality of work than those who didn't.

That said, there are some downsides to the Pomodoro Technique as well. For one thing, it may not be the best approach for tasks that require sustained concentration, like writing a long report or analyzing data. Interrupting your flow every 25 minutes can be disruptive and make it harder to stay focused.

Additionally, some people find the strict structure of the Pomodoro Technique to be a hindrance rather than a help. If you're the type of person who likes to work at your own pace and switch between tasks as needed, you may find the Pomodoro Technique too rigid.
Overall, the Pomodoro Technique can be a useful tool in your time management toolbox, especially if you struggle with focus or procrastination. But like any strategy, it's not one-size-fits-all.

Time batching - Time batching is a scheduling technique that involves grouping similar tasks together and completing them in a set amount of time. For example, you might dedicate a specific block of time to checking and responding to emails, followed by another block of time for completing a certain project.

One of the biggest advantages of time batching is that it allows you to focus on one type of task at a time, which can increase productivity and reduce distractions. It also helps you avoid the mental fatigue that comes with constantly switching between different types of tasks.

In fact, studies have shown that multitasking can actually decrease productivity and increase stress levels. One study found that employees who were interrupted by email or phone calls experienced a 20-25% reduction in productivity, and it took them an average of 15-20 minutes to return to their original task.

However, time batching can also have its downsides. For example, if you don't leave enough time between batches, you might find yourself rushing to complete tasks or feeling stressed if you don't finish everything on time. Additionally, it might not work as well for tasks that require constant attention or flexibility.

Overall, time batching can be a useful tool in time management, especially for tasks that are similar in nature. Just be sure to give yourself enough time between batches and be flexible in case unexpected tasks arise.

It seems daunting, but let's take it one day at a time. Try each technique each day, and find the one that works for you the best. It may take some getting used to, so maybe you'd even like to try one technique each week. No matter which technique of scheduling that you choose, time logging is a universal tool that helps keep track of your time and how you're feeling about it throughout each day.

Time logging involves tracking how you spend your time throughout the day. This technique helps you to identify patterns of time usage and find areas where you could be wasting time or procrastinating.

Think about your current approach to managing your time. Start by reflecting on your current habits and routines. What are some areas where you could be using your time more effectively? Are there any time-wasting activities or distractions that you could eliminate or reduce?

_____

_____

_____

_____

_____

_____

_____

Think about your priorities and goals. What are the most important tasks or activities that you need to accomplish this week? How can you make sure that you're devoting enough time and energy to these priorities?

_____

_____

_____

_____

_____

_____

_____

Consider different schedule techniques or tools that could help you manage your time more effectively. Do you prefer to use a paper planner or digital tool? Are there specific time management strategies that you'd like to try?

_____

_____

_____

_____

_____

Create a one-day schedule that takes into account your priorities, goals and preferred scheduling technique. If none of the ones above work for you, you can do your own research and find another one. Be realistic about how much time you need to accomplish different tasks, and build in buffer time for unexpected events or interruptions.

_____

_____

_____

_____

_____

_____

_____

_____

_____

_____

Finally, reflect on how your new time management schedule worked for you after you tried it for a day. Are you feeling less stressed and more in control of your time? What adjustments, if any, do you need to make to ensure that it's sustainable and effective long-term?

_____

_____

_____

_____

_____

_____

Breaking Tasks into Smaller Steps

It's like playing a game of "I Spy" with your to-do list, but instead of spying on objects, you're spying on tasks that can be broken down into smaller, more manageable pieces.

And guess what? This game is backed by science! Studies have shown that breaking down tasks into smaller steps not only makes them less overwhelming, but it also helps with time management. It's like hitting two birds with one stone, except we don't condone bird violence. But let's be real. The real reason why breaking down tasks is so great is that it makes you feel like you've accomplished something. It's like when you start a puzzle and complete the border, it feels like you're making progress, even though you still have hundreds of pieces left to put together. Not only will it reduce stress and help with time management, but it will also give you a sense of accomplishment. And who doesn't love feeling accomplished?

Let's take a larger task like planning a birthday party. This is how you could break it down:

1. Set a date and time for the party
2. Create a guest list
3. Choose a theme
4. Plan and prepare the decorations
5. Decide on the menu and make a grocery list
6. Purchase or gather all the necessary party supplies
7. Send out invitations or create an event on social media
8. Plan and organize party games or activities
9. Prepare cake and treats
10. Set up the party venue
11. Welcome and entertain guests
12. Clean up after it's over

Breaking down the task of planning a birthday party into smaller steps allows you to focus on one aspect at a time, making it feel more manageable and less stressful. You can then tackle each step sequentially, checking them off as you complete them, which provides a sense of accomplishment and motivation to keep going. Let's try to do it with a task in your life. Think of a task you have been putting off because it feels overwhelming.

_____

_____

_____

_____

Ask yourself what needs to be done first, then what comes next, and so on. Try to break it into between 5 and 10 steps. Consider the level of difficulty of each step and how much time you will need for each one.

_____

_____

_____

_____

_____

_____

_____

_____

_____

_____

Once you have broken down the task, schedule a time for each step and give yourself a deadline to complete the entire task. Reflect on the process and how breaking down the task into smaller steps helped you to approach it with less stress and more productivity.

_____

_____

_____

_____

_____

_____

_____

_____

_____

_____

_____

_____

_____

_____

Now that we've covered breaking tasks into smaller steps, it's time to focus on another important aspect of effective time management: limiting distractions. After all, what good is a well-planned schedule if we're constantly getting sidetracked by notifications, social media, or other interruptions? Let's dive into some strategies for minimizing distractions and staying focused.

Limiting Distractions

Distractions can be one of the biggest time-wasters, and when trying to manage time effectively and reduce overthinking, they can become a major obstacle. According to a study conducted by RescueTime, people spend, on average nearly three hours a day on their phone alone, which can severely cut into productivity and increase overthinking. By limiting distractions, we can create a focused environment that allows us to tackle tasks more efficiently and effectively. So, let's dive into some techniques to limit distractions and boost our time management skills.

It's all too easy to get sidetracked by distractions, whether it's social media, email notifications, or chatty coworkers. To manage your time more effectively, try to limit these distractions as much as possible. Turn off notifications on your phone, close unnecessary tabs on your computer, and find a quiet space to work if possible.

What types of distractions do you encounter regularly? Are there certain people, apps, activities that tend to distract you the most? How do you think they impact your productivity?

_____

_____

_____

_____

_____

_____

_____

Consider what contributes to these distractions. Are there certain times of day or environments that are more prone to distractions? How do your own habits and behaviors contribute?

_____

_____

_____

_____

_____

_____

_____

Brainstorm strategies for limiting distractions. What can you do to minimize interruptions and maintain focus on your work? How can you create an environment that supports your productivity?

_____

_____

_____

_____

_____

_____

_____

_____

Experiment with different strategies for limiting distractions. How effective are these strategies? Are there any adjustments you need to make?

_____

_____

_____

_____

_____

While it's important to set clear goals, prioritize tasks, and create a schedule, life can often throw unexpected curveballs at you. That's why being able to adapt and adjust your plans is a key skill for effective time management.

Being Flexible

Unexpected things can and will come up, so be prepared to adjust your schedule and priorities as needed. Don't beat yourself up if things don't go exactly as you planned.
Remember, progress is so much more important than perfection.

Being flexible is a crucial aspect of effective time management, especially for overthinkers who can get easily derailed by unexpected events or changes in plans. While techniques such as setting clear goals, prioritizing tasks, and creating a schedule are important, they can also create a rigid structure that can be difficult to maintain.

Being flexible allows us to adapt to unexpected situations, shift priorities as needed, and make the most of our time. In fact, research has shown that flexibility can increase productivity and reduce stress. A study published in the *Journal of Organizational Behavior* found that employees who had more control over their schedules and were allowed to be flexible with their time had higher job satisfaction and were more engaged at work.

For overthinkers, being flexible with their time can help reduce the anxiety that comes with feeling like they have to adhere to a strict schedule or plan. It allows them to take breaks when needed, adjust their workload to manage stress levels, and stay focused on what is most important.

Of course, being flexible doesn't mean being completely unstructured. It simply means allowing for some leeway and being open to change when it arises. By combining flexibility with the other time management techniques we've discussed, overthinkers can create a balanced approach that allows them to be productive while also taking care of their mental health. I know this may seem like a lot to juggle, so let's try to work through it if you're feeling overwhelmed. Brain break time!

Think about a recent day or week where you felt overwhelmed by your to-do list. Did you stick to your schedule rigidly or were you able to adapt as needed?

Reflect on how you felt during that time. Did your time management approach help or hinder your ability to manage your stress levels and reduce overthinking?

_____

_____

_____

_____

_____

_____

_____

_____

_____

Consider how you can incorporate more flexibility into your schedule while still prioritizing important tasks and avoiding distractions. Write down three specific ways you can be more flexible with your time management approach and how you think it will benefit your overall well-being.

_____

_____

_____

_____

_____

_____

_____

_____

_____

_____

_____

_____

_____

I know it can seem overwhelming, but we're going to take it one step at a time and accept any failures that may come our way. Sure, here's a section on giving ourselves empathy when we feel like we've failed at balancing flexibility and time management.

We all have days when we feel like we haven't accomplished anything, even when we've tried to balance flexibility and time management. It's easy to beat ourselves up for not sticking to our schedules or not being flexible enough when unexpected things come up. However, it's important to give ourselves empathy and understand that we're only human.

Research shows that self-compassion, or treating ourselves with kindness, is linked to greater psychological well-being and reduced stress levels. So, when we're struggling to find the balance between being flexible and managing our time, it's important to be kind to ourselves.

Try writing down some affirmations that remind you that it's okay to make mistakes and that you're doing your best. Examples might include: "I am human and I make mistakes," "I am doing the best I can with the time and resources I have," or "It's okay to adjust my schedule when unexpected things come up.

_____

_____

_____

_____

_____

_____

_____

_____

_____

_____

Remember, time management and flexibility are skills that take time to develop. It's okay if you don't get it right every time. The important things are to keep trying and to treat yourself with kindness and compassion along the way.

The Pitfalls of Time Management

If you made it through all those exercises, congratulations! You are on your way to being a master time manager. You're welcome. Before we continue, it's important to remember three major villains that will get in the way of your time management super skills: The Multitasker, The Workaholic and The Yes Man.

The Multitasker is the villain in your brain that tells you that you can accomplish multiple tasks at the same time. Contrary to popular belief, multitasking can actually be less efficient and more stressful than focusing on one task at a time. Try to just focus on the task at hand and avoid distractions like emails or social media until you're finished.

One of the main reasons why multitasking is so problematic is because it reduces the quality of your work. When we try to focus on multiple tasks simultaneously, it becomes challenging to give each task the full attention it deserves. When you constantly switch back and forth between tasks, your mind becomes overloaded and exhausted. This can lead to anxiety, feeling overwhelmed, and burnout, which can have a negative impact on your mental and physical health.

To avoid multitasking, it's essential to prioritize tasks and focus on one at a time. One effective strategy is to make a to-do list at the start of each day, ranking tasks by priority. This can help you stay focused on the most important tasks and avoid getting sidetracked by less essential ones.

It's important to give your brain and body time to rest and recharge. Schedule in regular breaks throughout your day and make sure to take time off to relax and do things you enjoy.

The Workaholic is the evil mastermind that manipulates you into thinking that you don't need to take breaks. When you work for long periods without taking a break, your energy levels decrease, making your productivity and efficiency suffer. Therefore, taking regular breaks is crucial to re-energize yourself and maintain focus. There are different types of breaks, including short breaks and longer ones, and each one serves a different purpose. Short breaks, such as taking a five-minute walk or doing a quick stretch, can help you break up your workday and avoid burnout. These short breaks can also help you recharge and refocus your attention on the task at hand.

Longer breaks, such as taking a lunch break or a midday nap, can help you rejuvenate yourself, reduce stress, and improve your health. These longer breaks give you the opportunity to recharge your battery, reflect on your goals, and come back to work with renewed energy and clarity.

It's important to remember that taking breaks is not a sign of laziness or unproductiveness. Instead, taking breaks is an essential part of staying productive and focused. To ensure that you're taking effective breaks, it's important to plan them in advance and stick to a schedule. Set aside specific times in your day for short and longer breaks, and make sure to use that time to rest, recharge, and rejuvenate. With proper breaks, you'll be able to achieve more, maintain your focus, and reduce your stress levels, which is the whole point of this chapter.

The Yes Man is the unrelenting guy that immediately says yes when anyone asks you to do something for them. Sometimes, the best way to manage your time is to say no to things that aren't essential or don't align with your priorities. Don't feel guilty about setting boundaries and saying no to requests that don't serve you.

Often, you may find yourself saying yes to requests, invitations, and opportunities without considering our own priorities and limitations. However, over-committing only contributes to the problem. Saying no can be challenging, especially if you don't want to disappoint others or appear uncooperative. However, it's important to remember that saying no is not a negative thing. Instead, it's an opportunity to prioritize your own needs, goals and well-being, and to make the most out of your time and energy.

One effective way to say no is to be honest and direct about your reasons. I know, your heart is already racing at the thought of being direct, or confrontational. For example, you can explain that you have other commitments or priorities that require your attention, or that you simply don't have the capacity to take on more responsibilities at the moment. You don't have to come up with an elaborate excuse or a lie that's 'good enough' for you to feel okay about saying no. You don't need to give the details; all you have to do is be direct about the fact that it simply doesn't fit into your schedule.

Another strategy, if you're more of a Type B, is to offer alternative solutions or compromises. For example, if you're asked to take on a task that you don't have time for, you can suggest someone who may be better suited for the task or offer to help in a different way. Learning to say no takes practice, and it's important to remember that it's a skill that can be developed over time.

Okay, so now you're wondering what all of this has to do with overthinking, right? Providing structure and organization to your day is a sure-fire way to reduce overthinking. When you have a clear plan for how you will use your time, you can focus more easily on the tasks at hand. Overthinking is bred out of anxiety. When you have a plan, your anxiety is lessened, and therefore your overthinking is also.

By prioritizing tasks and scheduling them into your day, you also reduce feeling overwhelmed. Again, overthinking is born from negative emotions, and being overwhelmed is included. When you have a plan in place, you can approach each task with greater clarity and focus, and good vibes = less overthinking.

Goals and priorities are another way to reduce overthinking. A common ANT (remember those?) of overthinkers is that they aren't going anywhere in life. Establishing clear, long-term goals reduces overthinking because you already know where you're going and what you're doing; you don't have to worry about it because it's already been planned. When you have a clear sense of what you want to achieve and how you will spend your time, you can make progress towards your goals with greater efficiency and effectiveness. Uncertainty and indecision will be blown away because of your stellar time-managing skills, blocking your brain from overthinking. Okay, so the formula is almost complete. We need one more ingredient to get rid of that overthinking for good: relaxation.

CHAPTER 6
LEARNING TO RELAX

You're almost to the end of this book, congratulations! By now, you should know that overthinking can be a real drag on your mental and emotional well-being. Hopefully you have gathered tons of useful tools to remedy your physical, mental, and emotional self as you've worked through these pages. It can feel like you're trapped in your own head, unable to escape the endless cycle of worry and rumination. This chapter is going to cover the last piece of the puzzle: relaxation. Relaxation techniques are similar to stress-relieving techniques, but have different goals.

Relaxation isn't just about finding a temporary relief from overthinking. It's about cultivating a deeper sense of well-being and resilience, equipping you for a resting state of calm. By practicing relaxation regularly, you can build up your emotional and mental muscles, ready to handle life's challenges with grace and ease, and more apt to implement your stress-relief techniques for when it all gets to be too much.

The following techniques might not all work for you, but the hope is that you can find at least one to practice routinely as part of your wellness. Let's start with yoga.

Yoga

Alright, let's get ready to stretch and bend like a pretzel! We're talking about yoga, the perfect relaxation technique for overthinkers who need to slow down their racing minds. Now, I know what you're thinking, "Yoga? That's just for hippies and contortionists!" But trust me, it's a lot more than that. Not only does yoga help improve your flexibility and balance, but it also reduces stress and anxiety levels.

In fact, a study published in the International Journal of Yoga showed that practicing yoga for just 12 weeks reduced symptoms of anxiety and depression in participants. That's right, just a few weeks of yoga can make a real difference in how you feel.

So, let's roll out our mats and get ready to say "Om." Even if you've never tried yoga before, don't worry! There are plenty of beginner-friendly poses and routines that will have you feeling like a yogi pro in no time. There are many different styles of yoga, each with its own focus and approach. Let's go through them:

Hatha Yoga: a gentle and accessible form of yoga that focuses on basic poses and breathing techniques. It's a great style for beginners, and also for anyone looking to build strength, increase flexibility, and promote relaxation.

The asanas are held for several breaths, and the emphasis is placed on proper alignment and breathing. It's a slower-paced style that allows you to tune into your body and focus on each movement and sensation.

Vinyasa Yoga: a dynamic and flowing style of yoga that emphasizes linking movement with breath. It's a more physically demanding style than Hatha, and it's great for building strength, flexibility and improving cardiovascular health.
In Vinyasa yoga, you'll move through poses in a flowing sequence, with each movement synchronized with an inhale and exhale. The sequence of poses can vary widely, depending on the teacher and class, but you can expect to move through a large variety.

Yin Yoga: A slow and more meditative style of yoga that focuses on holding passive poses for an extended period of time. You typically hold each pose for several minutes, allowing the body to sink deeper into the stretch and release any tension or tightness. The emphasis on letting go and surrendering to the pose, rather than actively working to achieve a specific posture.

Restorative Yoga: a gentle and relaxing style of yoga that focuses on resting the body and calming the mind. It's a great style for reducing your stress and nurturing your body. In this type of yoga, you'll use props such as blankets, bolsters, and blocks to support the body in passive poses for an extended period of time. The emphasis is on deep relaxation and surrender, rather than active stretching or strengthening.

Kundalini Yoga: a dynamic and transformative style of yoga that focuses on both physical and spiritual development. It's a style that people will use to increase energy, build strength and cultivate awareness.

In Kundalini, you'll use a combination of movement, breathwork and meditation to awaken and activate the energy at the base of the spine, channeling it upward through your body. This is thought to help clear energy blockages and promote a greater sense of well-being.

Remember, the key to practicing yoga is to listen to your body and go at your own pace. With regular practice, you may find that yoga becomes an important tool in your self-care routine and helps improve your relaxation. I know, I'm sure you've heard "just do yoga," as part of what you think is the stupidest advice ever, and I'm not trying to give you useless solutions to your real problems. However, I'm also going to say another thing you've heard before: don't knock it until you try it.

There are many different styles of yoga, and it's important to use one that resonates with you personally; yoga is not one size fits all. Yoga is just one tool in a broader toolkit for bringing you towards relaxation. What we can accept is that what you're doing now isn't working, hence the reason you've read this book. Pick one of the styles that resonate with you and your goals and try it out. Let's work through it:

What drew you to that style? How does it make you feel mentally when you picture it?

_____

_____

_____

_____

_____

Try it out and write about your experience. Follow a video tutorial or join a class that offers it. What challenges did you face when you practiced? Do you think you can do anything to overcome them?

_____

_____

_____

_____

_____

_____

_____

_____

Did you learn anything about yourself or your body? Did you discover any immense strengths or weaknesses?

_____

_____

_____

_____

_____

_____

_____

Would you like to continue? If so, what kind of support do you need to continue? Maybe a mentor, teacher, supportive community? Any additional resources?

_____

_____

_____

_____

_____

_____

_____

_____

_____

Maybe yoga isn't for you, or maybe you absolutely loved it. Either way, I'm proud of you for trying. Let's move onto something similar to try, Tai Chi.

Tai Chi

Are you looking for a relaxation technique that's a little more slow-paced and meditative than yoga? Look no further than tai chi! This ancient Chinese practice has been shown to help reduce stress and anxiety, improve balance and flexibility, and even lower blood pressure. Tai Chi is similar to yoga, but much less known as a relaxation technique. It's a gentle and flowing form of movement, often described as "moving meditation." It's based on the principles of traditional Chinese medicine, and is designed to promote a balanced sense of well-being.

Plus, tai chi is a low-impact exercise that's great for people of all ages and fitness levels. Its gentle, flowing movements help to calm the mind and release tension in the body, making it a perfect practice for overthinkers who need to unwind and let go of their racing thoughts. But don't just take our word for it - studies have shown that practicing tai chi regularly can have a positive impact on mental health. In one study, participants who practiced tai chi for 12 weeks reported feeling less anxious and depressed, and had lower levels of the stress hormone cortisol.

So, why not give tai chi a try? Find a local class or follow along with a video online to start experiencing the benefits of this calming and centering practice. Some common Tai Chi movements include the ones below. If anything, the names are super fun:

Cloud Hands: A fluid movement where you move your arms in a circular motion, as if you are holding a ball.

Wave Hands Like Clouds: A flowing movement where you shift your weight from side to side while moving your arms in a circular motion.

Grasp Sparrow's Tail: A series of movements that involve stepping forward and backward while moving your arms in a fluid motion.

These are just some of the things that you'll try once you start practicing. Again, I recommend trying everything to get a sense of what might work for you. Remember, the key to practicing Tai Chi for relaxation is to move slowly and mindfully, focusing on your breath and the sensations in your body.

How do you feel before you try Tai Chi?

_____

_____

_____

_____

_____

How did you feel after? Did you notice any changes in your physical or emotional state?

_____

_____

_____

_____

_____

_____

What did you find challenging about it? Were there any movements that you found frustrating or difficult?

_____

_____

_____

_____

_____

What did you enjoy? Did you find any movements that were relaxing or energizing?

_____

_____

_____

_____

What did you learn about yourself? Did you discover any strengths or areas to grow?

_____

_____

_____

_____

Do you want to incorporate Tai Chi into your weekly routine, and if so, what steps can you take to make it part of your self-care practice?

_____

_____

_____

_____

_____

Okay, maybe neither of those ones worked. What else can you do? Maybe you don't want to do anything physically taxing. So, let's get creative.

Art Therapy

Art therapy is a form of therapy that uses art-making as a way to help individuals process and express their emotions. It can be a really good tool for relaxation and self-care.

Art therapy can take many forms, including drawing, painting, sculpting and collage-making. The focus is on the process of creating rather than the finished product. The act of making art can be a meditative and calming experience, allowing individuals to focus on the present moment and tune out distractions.

It can also be used to explore difficult emotions and experiences in a safe and supportive environment. The leader may encourage you to create art that reflects your thoughts and feelings, and then help you process and make meaning of your artwork through discussion and reflection. Art therapy is basically a culmination of everything we've been working towards throughout this book. It covers all the things that contribute to your overthinking.

Reducing Stress: The act of making art can be a calming and meditative experience that will help you relax.

Promoting Self-Expression: Art therapy provides a safe and supportive space for you to express yourself creatively and explore your emotions.

Improving Mood: Creating art can be a source of joy and satisfaction, so say goodbye to ANTs! *Enhancing Mindfulness:* Art therapy encourages individuals to focus on the present moment and tune out distractions, which can promote mindfulness and inner peace.

Basically, art therapy is one-stop shop to all things wellness. But, this isn't to say that you won't struggle with it. Your overthinking will try its best to get in the way, but you have to battle it. As an overthinker, you're prone to a lot of self-doubt, which can make it difficult for you to allow yourself to create freely without judgment. You might worry about making mistakes or not creating something that's "good enough," hindering you from fully engaging in the creative process.

You also may struggle with analysis paralysis during art therapy, which means you'll get stuck in your head and over analyze every artistic decision that you make. This might make it difficult to let go and simply enjoy the process. Finally, with art therapy, you have to leave perfectionism at the door. It might be hard for you to fully embrace the imperfections and the messiness that can come with art-making. That's why art therapy is at the end of these suggestions, because you already have all the tools to overcome those feelings as you work through the art-making process.

Despite these potential challenges, art therapy can still be a valuable tool for you to explore and express your emotions. With the support of an art therapist, friend or family member, you can learn to overcome all of the pitfalls that you might run into. Tap into your creativity and relax! Once you've tried it, it's important to reflect on how you felt during the process. Take a few moments to reflect on your experience with art therapy. What feelings or emotions did you experience during your art-making process?

_____

_____

_____

_____

_____

_____

_____

_____

Did you notice any physical sensations in your body while you were working?

_____

_____

_____

_____

_____

_____

_____

_____

What thoughts or beliefs came up for you during the process?

_____

_____

_____

_____

_____

_____

_____

_____

Did you find it challenging to let go of self-judgment and embrace the creative process?

_____

_____

_____

_____

_____

What did you learn about yourself through this experience?

_____

_____

_____

_____

_____

_____

_____

_____

How do you feel now, after completing your art piece?

_____

_____

_____

_____

_____

Now, if these exercises feel overwhelming to you, you can always start small and build your way up to some more complicated ones. Let's talk about guided meditation. The power of technology is an amazing thing, and something that can be utilized for most things; relaxation is no different!

Guided Meditation

Guided meditation is a practice that involves using a guided recording or app to help you relax, focus your mind, and find inner peace. During a guided meditation, you'll be guided through a series of visualizations, breathing exercises, and relaxation techniques, often with the soothing voice of a meditation teacher leading you.

Guided meditation can be a powerful tool for reducing stress and anxiety, promoting relaxation, improving sleep quality, and boosting overall well-being. By focusing your mind on the present moment and cultivating a sense of calm, you can reduce the impact of negative thoughts and emotions, and increase feelings of positivity, mindfulness, and gratitude.
There are many guided meditation apps available that you can use to practice guided meditation. Some popular options include:

Headspace: Headspace is a mobile app that provides guided meditation sessions to help users reduce stress, improve focus, and promote better sleep. The app offers a variety of meditation programs tailored to different goals and levels of experience.

When you first sign up for Headspace, you can choose from a range of topics, such as stress, sleep, focus, and anxiety, as well as a duration for your session. The app then guides you through a series of breathing exercises and meditation techniques.

The sessions are led by a soothing voice that provides instructions and encourages you to stay present and focused. The app also includes animations and videos to help you better understand the concepts and techniques behind meditation.

Headspace also offers a range of other features, including sleep sounds, mindful movement exercises, and daily reminders to help you make meditation a regular part of your routine.

One of the main criticisms of the app is its cost, as a subscription is required to access many of its features

Calm: Calm is another popular app that provides guided meditation and relaxation techniques. The app features a variety of guided meditations, including ones for stress reduction, better sleep, and increased focus.

Like Headspace, Calm also offers both free and paid options. The paid version of the app provides access to a wider range of guided meditations, as well as other features such as bedtime stories, music, and breathing exercises.

One of the things that sets Calm apart is its visually stunning interface. The app features beautiful nature scenes and calming backgrounds, which can help create a peaceful and relaxing atmosphere.

Another benefit of Calm is its focus on relaxation techniques beyond just meditation. The app offers breathing exercises, mindfulness exercises, and even bedtime stories to help calm your mind and promote restful sleep.

However, one potential downside of Calm is that some users may find the paid version to be more expensive than other similar apps. Additionally, while the app's visuals are beautiful, they may not be to everyone's taste.

Insight Timer: Insight Timer is another popular meditation app that offers a variety of guided meditations, music, and talks from renowned meditation teachers. The app has a timer for self-guided meditation, and the ability to track progress over time. It also offers various categories of meditations such as mindfulness, stress and anxiety, sleep, and self-love, so you can choose what suits you best.

One of the great things about Insight Timer is that it offers a large library of free meditations, talks, and courses, with the option to upgrade to a paid subscription for more features. The app also allows you to connect with other meditators in the community and join group meditations.

However, some users have reported technical issues with the app and a lack of consistency in the quality of the meditations. Nonetheless, the app has received high ratings and positive reviews from many users.

Aura: Aura is another app that offers guided meditation for overthinkers looking to relax and calm their mind. The app features a variety of meditation sessions, including ones specifically designed for stress, anxiety, and sleep. One unique feature of Aura is that it uses artificial intelligence to personalize the meditations to each user's needs and preferences.

The app offers a free trial, after which users can choose to upgrade to a paid subscription for more content and features. The interface is easy to use and features a simple design, making it accessible to all users.

One of the biggest pros of Aura is its personalization feature. By taking into account the user's needs and preferences, Aura is able to offer meditations that are tailored to the individual, making them more effective in reducing stress and anxiety. Additionally, the app offers a variety of meditations, making it easy for users to find the right one for their needs.

On the downside, some users have reported technical glitches and bugs with the app. Additionally, the subscription cost may be a barrier for some users who are looking for a free app.

10% Happier: The 10% Happier app is another popular option for guided meditation. It was developed by ABC News anchor and meditation enthusiast Dan Harris, who discovered the benefits of mindfulness meditation after suffering a panic attack on air.

Similar to the other apps, 10% Happier offers a variety of guided meditations to choose from, ranging from beginner-friendly to more advanced. One unique aspect of the app is that it also includes video lessons from meditation teachers, as well as daily articles and podcasts on mindfulness and meditation.

One of the main benefits of the 10% Happier app is its focus on making meditation accessible and approachable for beginners. The app provides a clear and straightforward introduction to mindfulness meditation, without any of the mysticism or jargon that can sometimes turn people off.

However, some users have found the app's selection of guided meditations to be somewhat limited, particularly for more advanced practitioners. Additionally, while the video lessons and articles can be helpful, some users have found them to be less engaging than the content on other meditation apps.

Guided meditation can be done anywhere, anytime, making it an accessible and convenient way to promote relaxation. Like always, it's always important to reflect after you try something new. Use any of the apps that you're most drawn to, and only use the free version until you're sure that you like it.

Take a body scan. How did you feel before starting the guided meditation?

_____

_____

_____

_____

_____

What thoughts or feelings did you experience during the meditation? Did you notice any physical sensations in your body?

_____

_____

_____

_____

_____

_____

_____

_____

_____

_____

What impact did meditation have on your mood or overall sense of well-being? Write about your experience in as much detail as possible, reflecting on any insights or revelations you may have had during the meditation.

_____

_____

_____

_____

_____

_____

_____

_____

_____

_____

_____

_____

_____

_____

How did you feel after the meditation was over, and did you notice any changes in your thoughts or emotions throughout the rest of the day?

_____

_____

_____

_____

_____

_____

_____

_____

_____

What did you learn about yourself during this practice, and how can you incorporate guided meditation into your self-care routine moving forward?

_____

_____

_____

_____

_____

_____

_____

_____

_____

_____

_____

Self-Massage

Another quick, easy way to self-soothe is through self-massage. What a treat for the body and the mind! The benefits of self-massage are numerous, my friend. Not only does it feel amazing, but it can also reduce muscle tension, improve circulation, and relieve stress and anxiety.

Plus, it's free, and you don't need any fancy equipment or a partner to do it. Just your own two hands and a willingness to give yourself some much-needed love and attention.

Of course, there are a few downsides to self-massage. It can be tough to reach certain areas of the body, and it might not be as effective as getting a professional massage. But hey, it's still better than nothing!

And the best part? You don't need to take my word for it. There's actual scientific evidence to back up the benefits of self-massage. One study found that self-massage significantly reduced anxiety levels in patients with cancer, while another study found that self-massage improved circulation and reduced muscle fatigue in athletes.

So, what are you waiting for? Give yourself a nice rub down and feel the stress melt away. Just make sure to use some lotion or oil so you don't get any friction burns!

When you practice self-massage, it's important to tune into your body and listen to what it needs. Start by finding a quiet and comfortable space where you won't be disturbed, and take a few deep breaths to center yourself.

Next, choose an area of your body that feels particularly tight or tense, such as your neck, shoulders, back, or feet. Use your hands to apply gentle pressure to the area, using circular or sweeping motions to work out any knots or tightness.

If you're using a foam roller or massage ball, roll it slowly and mindfully over the area, applying gentle pressure and adjusting as needed to find the right level of intensity.

As you massage, pay attention to any sensations in your body, noticing where you feel tension or discomfort. Take deep breaths and try to relax your muscles as much as possible, allowing the massage to release any stress or tightness. Once you try it, don't forget to reflect: What techniques did you use, and what areas of your body did you focus on?

_____

_____

_____

_____

_____

How did your body feel before and after the self-massage practice? Did you notice any changes in your mood or overall sense of well-being?

_____

_____

_____

_____

_____

Write about your experience in as much detail as possible, reflecting on any insights or revelations you may have had during the practice. How did you feel after the practice was over, and did you notice any changes in your thoughts or emotions throughout the rest of the day?

_____

_____

_____

_____

_____

_____

_____

_____

_____

_____

_____

_____

_____

_____

_____

What did you learn about yourself during this practice, and if you enjoyed it, how can you incorporate self-massage into your self-care routine moving forward?

_____

_____

_____

_____

_____

_____

_____

_____

_____

_____

_____

Well, my dear reader, you've made it to the end of the chapter on relaxation techniques. Give yourself a pat on the back (or a self-massage, if you're feeling fancy) for making it this far.

I hope you've enjoyed learning about all these techniques for relaxing and reducing stress, because now you're officially equipped to handle any situation that comes your way. Stressed at work? Take some deep breaths. Anxious before a big presentation? Practice some guided meditation. Feeling sore after a workout? Give yourself a self-massage (or convince someone else to do it for you).

But in all seriousness, taking care of yourself and reducing stress is important. We all have busy lives and sometimes it can be hard to find time for self-care. But remember, you deserve to feel relaxed and at ease in your body and mind. So go ahead and try out some of these techniques, and see what works for you.

And if all else fails, there's always chocolate. (Kidding, but seriously, it does help sometimes.) And here's a bonus tip: Did you know that relaxation can actually help you control your thoughts? That's right, by taking some time to relax and clear your mind, you can stop those pesky thoughts from spiraling out of control.

So the next time you find yourself overthinking, just take a deep breath and imagine yourself on a beach, sipping a fruity drink and soaking up the sun. (Or if you hate the beach, imagine yourself in a cozy cabin in the woods, sipping hot cocoa and watching the snow fall. Whatever floats your boat.)

And if that doesn't work, just do some guided meditation and imagine yourself kicking those pesky thoughts right out of your brain. Bam! You've got this.

So go forth, my friends, and relax like it's your job. Because let's face it, in this crazy world we live in, sometimes the only way to survive is to just chill out and take a break. And who knows, you might even start to enjoy it.

EPILOGUE

Well, my fellow overthinker, you've made it to the end of this book. Congratulations! By now, you should be a pro at mastering your emotions, improving your time management skills, and turning negative thought patterns into positive ones. But how does all of this tie into overthinking, you ask?

Let me break it down for you. When we overthink, we tend to get stuck in a vicious cycle of negative thoughts and emotions. We obsess over every little detail, worry about things that haven't even happened yet, and drive ourselves crazy in the process. But by mastering our emotions, we can learn to control our reactions to these thoughts and prevent them from spiraling out of control.

And I can't express enough the importance of stress, the villain of your story. De-stressing is that magical activity that's supposed to make all of our worries and overthinking disappear. But does it really work? Well, according to science, it does. In fact, studies have shown that regular de-stressing activities, such as meditation, yoga, or even just taking a relaxing bath, can significantly reduce anxiety and help us manage our overthinking.

But who needs science, right? I mean, let's be real, what we really need is a sarcastic comment from our best friend or a funny meme to help us de-stress. Because sometimes laughter is the best medicine, even for overthinking. So go ahead, crack a joke, watch a funny video, or just let out a big, deep belly laugh. Your mind (and your abs) will thank you for it.

When it comes to time management, having a clear plan and structure for our day can help us avoid those moments of panic and anxiety that often lead to overthinking. By prioritizing our tasks and sticking to a schedule, we can stay focused and productive, rather than getting lost in our own thoughts.

But what about relaxation techniques, you ask? Well, my friends, these are your secret weapon against overthinking. When you feel yourself getting caught up in a cycle of negative thoughts, that's your cue to break out the deep breathing exercises, guided meditations, or even a good old-fashioned self-massage.

So, when should you use these relaxation techniques? Anytime, anywhere! Whether you're at work, at home, or on the go, there's always time to take a few deep breaths and center yourself. And the benefits? Reduced stress, improved mood, and a clearer mind that's better equipped to handle whatever challenges come your way.

So, my friend, take a deep breath and pat yourself on the back. You've come a long way, and you should be proud of yourself. Remember, you've got this, and with the right tools and mindset, you can overcome even the most persistent of negative thought patterns. Now go out there and live your best, least-overthinking life!

Made in the USA
Middletown, DE
09 July 2023

34798180R00087